# 10 Reasons Why America Will Fall

Michael Mebruer

Defiance Press & Publishing, LLC

# Contents

| | |
|---|---|
| Copyright | IV |
| 1. Foreword by Aaron Clarey | 1 |
| 2. Introduction | 4 |
| 3. Reason 1: Objective Reality Is Being Ignored | 10 |
| 4. Reason 2: Institutions Are Failing | 19 |
| 5. Reason 3: Modern Parents Suck | 43 |
| 6. Reason 4: Authoritarianism Has Arrived | 57 |
| 7. Reason 5: Young People Are Lied to About the Opposite Sex | 72 |
| 8. Reason 6: Societal Standards Have Fallen | 92 |
| 9. Reason 7: Men Are Checking Out | 98 |
| 10. Reason 8: There's No Personal Accountability | 114 |
| 11. Reason 9: People Act Terribly Because They Know They Can Get Away With It | 121 |
| 12. Reason 10: People Are Narcissistic | 129 |
| 13. Final Thoughts | 141 |
| 14. Works Cited | 148 |

10 REASONS THE UNITED STATES WILL FALL

Copyright © 2024 Michael Mebruer

(Defiance Press & Publishing, LLC)

Printed in the United States of America

10 9 8 7 6 5 4 3 2 1

All rights reserved. No part of this publication may be reproduced, distributed, or transmitted in any form or by any means, including photocopying, recording, or other electronic or mechanical methods, without the prior written permission of the publisher, except in the case of brief quotations embodied in critical reviews and certain other noncommercial uses permitted by copyright law.

This book is a work of non-fiction. The author has made every effort to ensure that the accuracy of the information in this book was correct at the time of the publication. Neither the author nor the publisher nor any other person(s) associated with this book may be held liable for any damages that may result from any of the ideas made by the author in this book.

ISBN- 978-1-963102-52-9 (Paperback)

ISBN- 978-1-963102-51-2 (eBook)

ISBN- 978-1-963102-53-6 (Hardcover)

Published by Defiance Press & Publishing, LLC, www.defiancepress.com

Bulk orders of this book may be obtained by contacting Defiance Press & Publishing, LLC, publishing@defiancepress.com

Public Relations Dept. – Defiance Press & Publishing, LLC, 281-581-9300

# Foreword by Aaron Clarey

When you consider a topic like "the inevitable demise of the United States," there's not a lot positive to say about it: The world's greatest country ever . . . that resulted in the most freedom ever . . . that single-handedly created more economic wealth and advancement than all empires and countries before it combined . . . is about to go away due to rank human laziness, stupidity, and envy. There is not much of a silver lining to point to.

But while Michael Mebruer's intention was to highlight the causes of the United States' inexorable decline in an effort to help people prepare for it, he has inadvertently painted more hope than he realized in this book. And this unexpected hope comes from the fact this book is written by a 20 something, not a sixty-year-old curmudgeon.

When my generation was in their 20s, they were thoroughly confident and smug; they knew everything. Their social science degrees convinced them they had all the solutions to all of society's problems. The media convinced them they would all be wildly happy, wildly in love, and wildly successful as they had finally unshackled themselves from the idiotic chains of tradition. The ultimate value one could have was blind devotion to parasitic leftist politics. And the most important thing about you was the genetic traits you were born with, not what you thought, did, accomplished, or achieved. We were on the precipice of achieving a utopia. And if any republican, libertarian, or free market naysayer said otherwise, they were to be immediately ostracized, called a racist or a sexist, and completely dismissed for daring to question the collective wisdom of this brilliant generation of 20 somethings.

Nearly thirty years later let me tell you about these once-brilliant 20 somethings. Most of them are overweight, ugly, and otherwise physically unattractive. They are divorced, often twice, even thrice, and have a bank account and estranged, tortured children to show for it. Many of them are on antidepressants or some other mind-altering drug. And none of them are on track to have an adequately funded retirement (many still shamefully having student loans for their know-it-all, sanctimonious degrees).

The few who are "successful" are largely so by feigning wealth through borrowing money to buy things they can't afford. They are slaves to their auto loans, student loans, third home equity loans, and credit cards, requiring they work as they abandon their children to daycare and public schools. And though our barren women have not an ounce of beauty or youth left in them, they still vainly try to cheat menopause through IVF, hormone treatment, or just dumb, blind hope. And what unfortunate children are born to these miserable people are diagnosed with a panoply of mental disorders—none of which are real—but conveniently mask the shitty parenting that is the cause.

And what of my generation's utopia?

Well, they got what they asked for. All the free money they clamored for has resulted in hyperinflation. Their children will never be able to afford homes or a life. The bill for their arrogance has been tallied in the national debt, which at best will be repaid by their children or through even more inflation which will make retirement impossible. And in their blind, complete and whole dick-sucking of a socialist economic system, they've made it so we as a nation are incapable of producing what we need to survive (though if you need a sermon on the evils of racism from someone with their Masters in Diversity and Inclusion, we have those people in spades). But perhaps the worst thing they did to America is they turned men and women against each other, depriving their own (and future) generations of the one thing that would make life worth living – love (though there are plenty of lippy, fat chicks and soy boy democrat men if you're willing).

These people were not only wrong about pretty much everything, but they wasted their lives believing in their own bullshit. And to be perfectly honest, most of them might as well end their lives because not only have they been veritably worthless people up until now, it is doubtful what remains of their futures will be anything but pain.

But Mike's generation is different. And this is evidenced in his book.

Not that all modern day 20 somethings are as savvy and aware as Mike, but they are infinitely more aware of today's problems than my generation of know-it-all peers who were binging on *Friends* in the 90s. Young people today *are* aware of inflation. Young people today *are* aware of the stupidity and inefficiency of college. Young people *are* distrustful of the "adults" who run the country. And young men and women of today are *acutely* aware of the raging war of the sexes going on today. And whereas Mike's book would have fallen on deaf ears if it were written thirty years ago, today young people might actually heed it as they have infinitely more street smarts than their boomer and Gen X peers ever did.

This book no doubt paints a dire and grim picture of the future of the United States, but it does point it out to an audience who *may* do something about it. And while for seasoned, curmudgeonly old timers such as myself, this writing has always been on the wall; young people of today may actually do something about it and make it so they don't piss away their lives like my generation did.

-Aaron Clarey

# Introduction

America is a great and wonderful place, founded on the ideals of freedom and personal liberty. It is one of the greatest and most powerful societies in human history. I am not an idealistic sixteen-year-old who believes that America is flawless in its existence. But I would argue that the evils that America engaged in were not unique to America. And most of what makes America good is unique to America.

An example of an evil is that America allowed the institution of slavery to exist. That is something that will always be a stain on our legacy. And rightfully so. Slavery is an institution that denies the very humanity of its victims because it allows one human to own another, reducing the victim to nothing more than property. Unfortunately, slavery has existed in nearly all societies throughout human history.

What makes America unique is the price she paid to get rid of slavery. America fought a bloody civil war that cost the lives of over 600,000 Americans.[40] It was done so that we could live up to the original promise in the Declaration of Independence: "We hold these truths to be self-evident, that all men are created equal, that they are endowed by their Creator with certain unalienable Rights, that among these are Life, Liberty and the pursuit of Happiness"[41].

I don't think there has been a greater force for global freedom. Wherever the United States goes, freedom follows. For starters, the United States protected South Korea and Western Europe from communist influence. That is why these areas remained free throughout the twentieth century. When America leaves, freedom goes with it. Look at the fall of South Vietnam in the 1970s, or the way Afghanistan was left to the Taliban in 2021.

It's more than America spreading global freedom that makes it a truly wonderful country. I would argue that America is more than a nation. It is an idea, an amazing one that spans all cultures, races, and languages. American freedom acts as a beacon for people across the world. I went to primary school with people from Mexico, Guatemala, and Germany. I studied economics with a Kuwaiti. And I have worked with people from the Philippines, India, and Rwanda. These people came to America and made it their home. And since none of them ever asked me to play soccer, I think they assimilated pretty well.

My family wasn't among the first to settle America. Like so many others, my ancestors left their homelands in search of a better life. My family tree shows that my ancestors were originally from Germany and Poland. It wasn't until the 1800s that the first recorded Mebruer was documented in St. Louis.

Migration is the most powerful measurement of a good society: People are leaving everything that they have and know to start somewhere else. This is why I have never taken seriously the idea that, "America is an oppressive place." It wouldn't make sense for people to leave everything that is familiar only to willingly walk into their own oppression.

There is a reason why Cubans would attempt to float to America on makeshift rafts. By contrast, I don't think Bernie Sanders was ever that desperate to get to Cuba. The American flag has become a symbol of freedom. That's why Hong Kong protesters flew American flags in the face of Chinese Communist oppression.

Contrary to what some people on the far right believe, American ideals can be found among peoples across the world. You do not need to be born in America to truly embody the American spirit. In fact, I would argue that some first-generation immigrants are more American than some people who were born here.

A good example is a friend of mine, a first-generation Indian immigrant. His parents sent him to the United States for college. He studied and worked hard. He eventually became an oncologist and a damn good one at that. He showed deep compassion for his patients and was well loved in the community where he worked. I would say that he embodied the American spirit. By that, I mean he worked hard, made his own way, and didn't demand that the rest of society pay his way. He certainly embodied Americanness more than the entitled West Coast communist wannabes like Hasan Piker, the type of people who will rant about the excesses of capitalism and call themselves socialists. And yet live in a $2.75 million mansion in Los Angeles.[42]

That brings me to the topic of this book. America is falling, and I believe that we are past the point of no return. I don't believe that there is any one reason for America's decline. There are many cultural and political reasons for it.

American ideals are being abandoned. Values such as individual rights and limited government are being tossed aside for attempts at a utopia that cannot exist. The rise in socialism in the United States is the greatest example of this. According to Pew Research,[43] in 2022, 36% of U.S. adults had a somewhat positive view of socialism (30%) or a very positive view of socialism (6%). While it is a decline from a 2019 poll that showed 42% of Americans viewed socialism favorably, parts of the survey are alarming. Forty-four percent of young adults aged 18–29 had a favorable view of socialism. People age 65 and older viewed capitalism more favorably than socialism (73% had a positive view of capitalism and 28% had a positive view of socialism). And 57% of Democrats surveyed had a favorable view of socialism. Most major American political parties have a positive view of socialism.

America has always been a nation that idealizes the rights of the individual. Most of the U.S. Constitution is designed to protect the rights of individuals by limiting governments at the state, local, and federal levels.

This is antithetical to socialism. A socialist society, one that only cares about the collective, does not have any concern for the rights of the individual. It's not like the Khmer Rouge had respect for the rights of Cambodian civilians in the 1970s. After all, they only killed a million Cambodians. And if you ever want to see what individual rights mean in a collective-based society, read *The Gulag Archipelago* by Aleksandr Solzhenitsyn. He tells stories about how Soviet civilians were arrested for ridiculous reasons.

One of the wilder stories was about how most members of a Soviet family were arrested. A husband and wife were arrested for a minor charge. They probably received a ten-year sentence in a work camp because of the crime. However, their infant child was left behind. A neighbor noticed that the infant was alone and took the child to the police station. She inquired about what to do with the child and wondered who would take care of the baby since the parents had been arrested. For her compassion, she was arrested. And proclaiming your innocence wouldn't do any good, the state would torture a confession out of you.

If you must provide a good or service against your will, you will provide that good for the betterment of the collective. If you are successful, your gains will be seized and redistributed for the betterment of the collective. This even happens in capitalist societies, it's called "progressive tax systems." Even in the United States, politicians like Elizabeth Warren have talked about instating "wealth taxes."

If you speak your mind, and it is offensive to others, you will be censored for the betterment of the collective. In 2023, a woman was arrested for silently praying in a restricted zone. If you heard about this, you would probably think that this happened in China or North Korea. Wrong. It happened in the UK.[44]

So, what does the fall of America look like? Well, there are a lot of possibilities. I don't think that America is going to sink into the ocean, despite what Al Gore believes.

I don't believe that the United States would ever fall to a foreign invader. Our geographic location and the size of our country would make it very difficult to land an invasion force, let alone actually seize United States territory by force. It could mean that the American hegemony could end. The American hegemony is our status as the dominant power among our allies. As the American hegemony fades, our status as the global superpower will collapse. While this may sound good for some people, they don't know what will replace the American hegemony. Also, the American people have been accustomed to being the economic superpower. What if the Chinese were able to replace the United States as the global superpower? You would see a world order that is not concerned with freedom and would use any means to consolidate power. Consolidating power is one reason why China seeks to absorb Taiwan. It produces over 60% of the world's semiconductors and over 90% of the most advanced ones.[45]

The most likely scenario is that the United States will ultimately succumb to socialism. It may seem strange to think this. After all, America triumphed over socialism in the 1990s when the Soviet Union collapsed. The argument between socialism and capitalism was supposedly settled. But socialism is like cancer, and cancer can always come back around. And the Pew Research poll I mentioned earlier, showed that socialism is popular among American youth. I thought socialism was interesting at one point. I was sixteen. It wasn't that I was stupid. I just didn't know anything.

I like what conservative author and political commentator Andrew Klavan once said about the fall of America. Klavan is a down-to-earth guy, who can add humor and sarcasm to his shows and podcasts, but I remember this subject because he was serious, and yet not bothered by it. Klavan said something along the lines of, "I do believe that socialism will win the day in America. Because all things ultimately die, and this will signify the death of America." Even if American society is still functional at that point, it would be a disservice to call that society "America" because everything that was instrumental to American society would be gone. The rights and responsibilities of the individual are the most important aspect. The individual was free to be the author of his or her own story. The individual would reap the benefits of his or her successes and that same individual would pay for his or her failures. Charles Murray gave a good summation of the way American society was meant to operate. "But the American project was not about maximizing national wealth nor international dominance. The American project ... consists of the continuing effort, begun with the founding, to demonstrate that human beings can be left free as individuals and families to live their lives as they see fit. Coming together voluntarily to solve their joint problems"[130]. Without this focus on the individual, we will simply be left with a perversion of what America once was and a perversion of everything that made it great.

America will no longer be a beacon of freedom and opportunity. America will lose both on its path toward a perfect and equal society. And by equal society, I mean equality of outcome, not equality of opportunity.

And the worst part is that the American people would sign off on the death of America. To be fair, Americans won't see proposals to kill America on a ballot. However, the people we have elected, and the policies they enacted have deeply wounded America, and America is bleeding out as a result. The most damaging policy is that of massive deficit spending that will result in fiscal collapse. More of this in Chapter 2.

Regardless of what an American fall looks like, it will be felt around the world. And it will be a tragedy that befalls all mankind. But enough of what the theoretical fall will look like. Let me tell you *why* we will fall.

# Reason 1: Objective Reality Is Being Ignored

"Reality is that which, when you stop believing in it, doesn't go away."

–Philip K. Dick

Objective: expressing or dealing with facts or conditions as perceived without distortion by personal feelings, prejudices, or interpretations.[1]

In my career as a medical laboratory technician, focusing on objective goals and reasoning is the foundation of my job. My duties consist of running patient samples and ensuring the accuracy of the results. We follow procedures for everything we do. All of this is done to ensure valid results.

For example, one of the most common errors in healthcare is treating the wrong patient. I have heard of young women getting unnecessary hysterectomies due to patient misidentification. So, when we draw blood from a patient, we use two-step patient identification. There are different ways of achieving two-step patient identification. For outpatients, we asked the patient to state their name and date of birth. If it's a patient in the hospital, the patient will have a wristband with their necessary information. We do this to ensure that the results go to the proper patient.

Another way that we ensure accurate results is by running quality control (QC) on our instruments. Quality control is a known value that we run on a machine, and we need to get a result that is in an acceptable range. If a QC result is outside the acceptable range, it is necessary to perform corrective action to get the results back in range. Several types of corrective action can be performed, depending on the machine. Typically, the first thing you do is rerun the QC. If that doesn't work, there are several things to try. Options can range from changing reagent packs, performing maintenance, trying a new QC sample, or recalibrating the machine.

But what you cannot do under any circumstances is say, "I feel that the machine is fine" and then resume running patient samples with unacceptable QC results. Your feelings do not matter; what matters is ensuring the accuracy and validity of lab results. Your subjective feelings have no way of verifying results. In fact, basing your work in objective reality can mean the difference between life and death.

Everything we do from the time we draw the blood, to when we give the nurse the donated pack of blood for the patient transfusion, is documented. And every step is written in a procedure to ensure clarity of proper protocol. There is no room for subjective feelings because that can lead to a disaster.

Let's say that you have a patient that is O positive. You don't get to say, "Well I feel like the patient is A positive. Blood types are just a product of the white patriarchy. And Karl Landsteiner (the man who discovered major blood types) was a beneficiary of the privileges of society, so what does he know about blood types?" You can engage in as much wordplay and mental gymnastics as you want, but the fact remains; you can't give type A blood to a person with type O blood. Why not? A person with type O blood has Anti-A antibodies in their bloodstream. It will cause a fatal transfusion reaction.

What makes objective reality so important is that it is common ground for everyone to agree on. You can take two lab techs working 1,000 miles apart. The objective reality of the job gives them common ground. It's why any competent technician will tell you that you cannot give type A donated blood to a patient with type O blood.

There is a scene in George Orwell's *1984*, where the protagonist Winston Smith is tortured by a member of the state. In it the statesman tries to convince Smith that two plus two equals five if the state says so. Smith asks, "How can I help it? How can I help but see what is in front of my eyes? Two and two are four."

The torturer says, "Sometimes, Winston. Sometimes they are five. Sometimes they are three. Sometimes they are all of them at once."

Of course, this is total garbage. You can redefine four to mean five and five to mean four. But you can't change what the numbers represent. There's a reason why objective reality transcends languages. People who speak Spanish understand this sense of objective reality. After all, *dos mas dos es cuatro*.

Some people have tried to dismiss objective reality as a form of bigotry. Some people have gone so far as to say that math is racist. In 2019, Seattle educators suggested that a new type of math be taught. "Students will be taught how "Western Math" is used as a tool of power and oppression, and that it disenfranchises people and communities of color. They will be taught that "Western Math" limits economic opportunities for people of color. They will be taught that mathematics knowledge has been withheld from people of color."[46]

Some people think having an objective standard when it comes to teaching English is racist. As Asao Inoue, a professor at Arizona State University, once said, "If you use a single standard to grade your students' languaging, you engage in racism. You actively promote white language supremacy, which is the handmaiden to white bias in the world." [47]

Don't be fooled by educators like these. They do not seek to alleviate racism in our society; they are more than willing to push racist narratives if it suits their needs. All they seek to do is to limit objective terms, so that they can dominate the language. And as we all know from the history of totalitarianism, dominating the language often means dominating the people.

Two terms that have been nearly reduced to nothing are the terms "man" and "woman." Once it was biologically clear what a man and a woman were. But now the two terms have become convoluted, with any objective basis being cast aside for subjective feelings. A depressing yet hilarious example of this is a headline from the *Daily Mail*. The headline reads: "TRANS WOMAN IS CLEARED OF FLASHING HER PENIS AT THREE WOMEN USING OHIO YMCA AFTER JUDGE RULED SHE'S TOO FAT FOR HER GENITALS TO BE VISIBLE." [48]

Today people try to redefine terms to suit their own narratives. But redefining a term does not change the reality that it represents. *Cambridge*

*Dictionary* defines a woman as "an adult female human being," which sounds reasonable. But what is the definition of female? According to *Cambridge Dictionary*, female is defined as "belonging to or related to women." So, what you end up with is a circular logical fallacy. It leads to someone saying, "I am a woman. I know this because I am a female. And I know that I am a female because I am a woman."

You will see this a lot if you ever watch the documentary *What Is a Woman?* The host, Matt Walsh, asks numerous people, "What is a woman?" He asks women, social scientists, psychologists, and activists, but no one really has an answer. Most people default to subjective feelings. One of the more ridiculous answers was something along the lines of "a woman is what you feel it is," which essentially says, if you feel like you're a woman, you are one.

Considering an individual's feelings is not a proper way to classify something. When you categorize something, there must be standards, and these standards are exclusionary by nature. This is something that scientists have done when distinguishing organisms from one another. There are various levels of classification. The levels start at the broadest, and the scope narrows as you progress down the levels of classification. Going from broadest to most specific, the levels are kingdom, phylum, class, order, family, genus, and species. This method of classification is how you can distinguish humans from something like a catfish.

A catfish belongs to the "fish" class. Fish have gills; they lay eggs, and they are cold blooded. These are just three distinguishing characteristics of the fish class; and there are other properties. But all three of these features exclude humans from the group. Humans have lungs, give birth to live young, and they are warm blooded. It is not discriminatory to say that a human is not a fish; it is simply stating the reality of the objective classification.

Objective classification does not stop at distinguishing different types of animals. It is also a way of distinguishing the sex of a specie. It's something that we can do and have done for humans.

For example, a human male will have XY sex-linked chromosomes. Males do not have the capacity to give birth. This is because male gametes are sperm cells. On the other hand, females have XX sex-linked chromosomes. The female gamete is the egg cell. Because of this, females are the sex that has the capacity to give birth. For a more in-depth look at the differences between men and women from an evolutionary point of view, I recommend reading *The Ape That Understood the Universe* by Steve Stewart-Williams.

If I were to be asked, "What is a woman?" My response would be "an adult human female." And I would define "man" as an "adult human male." These two classes are mutually exclusive. A potential exception would be the rare example of humans suffering from rare, genetic abnormalities. So, if you've ever read an article claiming that a man has given birth[50], you know that the article is a lie. It's actually a woman who calls herself a man. Whoever wrote the article is trying to push a subjective gender ideology.

It's surprising that people have bought into these ridiculous ideologies. But it's even more surprising who has bought into the ideologies. I always found it strange that homosexuals include people in their movement that believe in trans ideology. This is because people who believe in trans ideology try to do everything possible to blur the lines between men and women. But the distinction between men and women is key for the homosexual identity.

I don't have any problem recognizing the homosexual identity. In fact, I can objectively define and classify homosexuals. Since I have already defined what a woman is, I can define what a lesbian is. A lesbian is a woman who is sexually attracted to other women: It's a basic but accurate definition. I can also objectively define what a homosexual man is: a man sexually attracted to other men. I have been able to objectively define and classify individuals that belong to these groups. By this classification, a male (man) cannot be a lesbian and a female (woman) cannot be a homosexual man. I know that this all seems basic, but some transactivists in our society completely deny these classifications. And what's more, they will accuse someone of bigotry for holding to these standards of classification.

In April 2023, left-wing commentator Ana Kasparian received online criticism for not wanting to be referred to as a "birthing person" and said this term was degrading to women. Activists accused Kasparian of being a TERF (trans exclusionary radical feminist) and toxic.[49]

As I said above, people who push radical gender ideology try to blur the lines between men and women. These people will say that a man can call himself a woman and become a lesbian if he is sexually attracted to women.

Since these people have reduced the terms *men* and *women* to the whims of subjective feelings, the terms have lost all meaning.

If anyone can claim to be a woman, then anyone can claim to be a lesbian. And if that's the case, how do you distinguish a lesbian from a heterosexual man? Sure, you can simply ask the person if he/she is a lesbian, but because there is no objective classification, the term "lesbian" means nothing. It has become a blanket term that can mean anything depending on whom you talk to. And because terms such as man and woman are meaningless in this context, the terms "lesbian" and "homosexual man" are also meaningless, meaning the homosexual identity has been destroyed in this scenario.

It's not just the gay community that has been harmed by this subjective ideology. Some of the saddest stories are of people who identified as trans but stopped the transitioning process later in life. Many of them stopped after taking artificial hormones or receiving permanent surgeries. And these artificial hormones and surgeries are things that medical professionals are pushing on young people.

There are now medical institutions that are pushing "puberty blockers," meaning they are designed for teens and preteen children. Some of these drugs (such as Lupron) were once used to chemically castrate sex offenders. I'll talk about these doctors in later chapters, but to keep with the theme of this chapter, I'd like to reiterate that objective reality is being ignored. There are teenagers who feel uncomfortable in their bodies. It's not surprising because puberty can be a difficult time for kids. Many teenagers have a level of discomfort with their body in one way or another.

I can't say what puberty is like for a girl, but I can say that they have their unique problems. I say these are unique because contrary to what the *Guardian* says, men can't get pregnant. In 2019, the *Guardian* published an article titled, "The Dad Who Gave Birth: 'Being Pregnant Doesn't Change Me Being a Trans Man.'"[50] I may be speaking from my own experience here, but my father had five kids. And he didn't give birth to any of them. The "man" in the *Guardian* article was a woman who called herself a man. And her biology didn't care what she identified as.

In the early 2000s, there was a lot of talk about the dangers of eating disorders and the adverse effects they can have. Those messages are geared toward women.

The problem is that instead of reassuring the child and understanding that what they're going through is probably a phase, many institutions suggest that the child is a member of the opposite sex and indulge in that delusion.

Abigail Shrier wrote an article in *City Journal*[51] that outlined the struggle of a Pakistani family with their son. Ahmed's son was giving credible threats of suicide, so Ahmed took him to the Seattle Children's Hospital. It's worth noting that Ahmed's son was sixteen and on the autistic spectrum. When Ahmed received updates from the hospital, the hospital referred to Ahmed's son as his "daughter." Medical workers said, "We had calls with counselors and therapists in the establishment, telling us how important it is for him to change his gender, because that's the only way he's going to be better out of this suicidal depressive state."[52] And because Ahmed's son was sixteen, he could receive gender-affirming care. In the state of Washington, children as young as thirteen can receive gender-affirming care without parental consent. Fortunately, Ahmed stayed calm and pretended to go along with the plan to transition his son. Once he had his son, Ahmed quit his job and moved his entire family out of Washington. When Shier followed up with Ahmed's family, Ahmed said that his son was no longer suicidal or transgender.

It's one thing for an adult to have some sort of delusion. Some adults seek to transition through surgeries and hormone therapy. Adults are capable of consent, but consent does not always mean that something is right. These people face serious mental issues that go beyond body dysmorphia. Anxiety and depression are two common symptoms of people with gender dysphoria. If these people are suffering from mental illness, the mental illness should be treated rather than encouraging a delusion. I would ask three questions of people who encourage gender transition: Can a person be truly happy while living in a delusionary state? Is it fair to make the rest of society cater to the delusions of a mentally ill population? Would it be acceptable to encourage the excesses of people with bipolar personality disorder while they are on a manic high?

It is another matter entirely when dealing with kids because they typically lack the knowledge and experience to deal with the real world. It's unacceptable that institutions ranging from governments to school systems are allowing these harmful delusions to go unchecked. It's hard to believe that adults think that children can make these choices.

The problem is not that the child was born into the "wrong body." Every part of what you are and what you are going to be is written in your DNA. If you were supposed to be a boy, you would have an XY sex linked chromosome. And no matter how many surgeries you get or how many hormones you take, that fact will never change.

The real problem is the discomfort that people are having in their own bodies. There could be a range of reasons for this discomfort, but I have often wondered how many of these people have had some sort of traumatic experience. Many of them suffer from depression and mental illness. Instead of trying to get to the root cause of the depression or mental illness, it has often become standard practice to do everything possible to make the delusion a reality even if the delusion is a symptom and not the root cause.

In one of the crazier examples in our culture, take the example of a woman who had a desire to be blind. She claimed that she had wanted to be blind since childhood. She talked to a psychiatrist about her issues, but the psychiatrist decided that it would be beneficial for her to blind herself. With the assistance of the psychiatrist, the woman poured drain cleaner in her eyes causing massive amounts of damage. The woman eventually went blind from this. She did all of this because she felt that she was *supposed* to be blind.[52]

While that is one of the wilder examples of being uncomfortable with one's own body, it is becoming common for subjective feelings to take precedent over objective reality. Look at the exponential rise in transgender and nonbinary people in populations over the last few years. According to a 2022 Pew Research study, "Adults under 30 are more likely than older adults to be trans or nonbinary. Some 5.1% of adults younger than 30 are trans or nonbinary, including 2.0% who are a trans man or trans woman and 3.0% who are nonbinary – that is, they are neither a man nor a woman or aren't strictly one or the other. (Due to rounding, subtotals may not add up to the total.) This compares with 1.6% of 30- to 49-year-olds and 0.3% of those 50 and older who are trans or nonbinary."[53]

Reality doesn't care about your feelings. Reality is like a freight train moving toward you. Whether or not you acknowledge it is irrelevant. Reality will smack you square in the face, and the more you try to fight it, the harder it will be. Two plus two is not five. Tigers are not herbivores.

Men are not women and women are not men. Categories and classifications are naturally exclusive. If you do not meet the criteria, then you are not part of the group.

It does not matter how you feel. If you are a man, you are not a woman. You cannot become a woman. You will never be a woman. You can have as many surgeries and medications as you want: You will simply be a man with the appearance of a woman. You can have all of society indulge your delusion, but it will never change the fact that you are not a woman.

We should not be in the business of indulging people in their delusions because reality will win every time. And the people who tried to deny reality will pay a huge price. Many people have bought into radical gender ideology. Many of them started when they were kids. They took puberty blockers and tried to socially transition themselves. And because people did not push back on their delusions, these people caused irreversible damage to their bodies. Even when they decided to identify as their original gender, they still had to deal with the damage. Many people must deal with sterility. Serious harm has been done to these people because American society has decided that objective reality doesn't matter. All that matters is one's feelings, even when one's feelings can change with time.

# Reason 2: Institutions Are Failing

"Let me start off with two words. 'Made in America.'"

—Joe Biden

Many institutions in America are on the brink of failing. People fail for different reasons. But most failing institutions are caused by the self-serving, incompetent fools running these institutions. Three critical institutions are failing the United States: our leadership (our political class), our education system, and American families.

An increasing number of institutions are falling. Legacy media is one that deserves an honorable mention. Trust in the media is extremely low. A Gallup poll showed that in 2021, trust in the media was at near record lows. The poll showed that only 34% of the people surveyed had a "great deal" or "fair amount" of confidence in media.[2] And it's not like this distrust is unwarranted.

One of the things that still amazes me, is that media figures were upset when people protested the COVID lockdowns, but then those same media figures supported large crowds of people at Black Lives Matter rallies. When those protests turned violent, the media called the riots "mostly peaceful protests." An infamous example of this sort of coverage could be seen in the Kenosha BLM riots following the shooting of Jacob Blake. A CNN reporter was reporting on the riot. As cars and buildings burned in the background, the CNN chyron read "FIERY BUT MOSTLY PEACEFUL PROTESTS AFTER POLICE SHOOTING." The media deserves the level of mistrust[151].

However, I don't believe that corrupt media institutions will be the downfall of the United States. New forms of media and other news alternatives can rise from the ashes of the former media. The market has ways of dealing with outdated and untrusted media sources. The same can be said for most institutions that face decay. If a bank decides it wants to focus on virtue signaling their DEI (diversity, equity, and inclusion) hiring practices and not worry about its investors, then those banks can enjoy the eventual collapse that comes with it. In 2023, Silicon Valley Bank (SVB) faced financial collapse. SVB did not have a chief risk officer for several months in 2022.[54] According to the *Insurance Journal*, "SVB revealed in a 2023 proxy statement that Chief Risk Officer Laura Izurieta left the company in October but stopped performing the role in April. The company said Kim Olson took over the job in December"[132]. SVB went approximately eight months without a Chief Risk Officer. If SVB had one, they would have seen the liquidity issues the bank was facing.

Risk management and liquidity issues may not have been important, but do you know what SVB had time for? Diversity, equity, and inclusion (DEI), which pretty much means affirmative action practices that SVB can virtue signal about. As SVB said in a memo on Diversity, Equity, and Inclusion, "We have a commitment to addressing social oppression in all its forms (racism, heterosexism, ageism, ableism, low socio-economic backgrounds, etc.), with a focus on Black, Latinx, and gender representation (groups underrepresented in the innovation economy)"[55]. The purpose of a bank is to keep the money of its clients safe and easily accessible. If banks like SVB want to play social justice warrior and shirk their main responsibilities, then they can enjoy going under. There are plenty of other banks to choose from.

However, the institutions in this chapter have no substitute. There are no proper market substitutions for the American government, the education system, and the family unit. The American government's job is to "fill the gaps" the private sector does not fill—to take societal cost and benefit into consideration.

The public education system is not needed by everyone. Middle- and upper-income families can afford to send their kids to private school, or they can homeschool their kids. However, low-income families are the ones who need some public education option for their children because they don't have the funds for private school. American public schools are in desperate need of reform.

The family unit is arguably the most important institution because it is responsible for raising the next generation of kids to a responsible adulthood. However, the family unit is falling, and younger generations are suffering. You will see more of this in Chapter 3. Once these institutions fall, Americans will pay a large price.

Leadership

Out of everything that I mentioned in this book, our country's leadership will doom America more than anything else. When I was a kid, I had the idea that the people in our government were highly skilled and competent. And it's not hard to see why I thought that: People in the government are often well-dressed, well-spoken, and many of them have an Ivy League education. But that's the thing about getting older. I began to realize that the people in charge are corrupt, incompetent, and self-serving. Maybe not everyone, but enough to screw things up.

Learning about economics was one of the things that opened my eyes to the lies and incompetence of government officials. It always frustrates me when I hear some government officials say, "We created X number of jobs." Or when Obama was talking down to rich people in his famous, "You didn't build those roads" speech. Looking at it now, Obama was right. Rich people did not go out and build the public roads that we drive on. But they sure paid for it. We don't owe Obama or the government anything. Why? Because Obama and government officials didn't pay for those roads. They simply took other people's money and spent it on what they thought was beneficial. And then they have the audacity to expect me to be grateful to them for taking my money.

I would also like to note that the government does not create anything. The government simply redistributes resources from one sector of the economy to another.

The United States measures economic growth through Gross Domestic Product (GDP). The most basic formula to calculate GDP is through the following: consumption spending + investments + government spending + net export (C+I+G+NX). From this formula, you notice that government spending is part of GDP. The problem is that you do not see the variables that affect each part of the equation.

Where does government spending come from? Taxes. In more advanced and detailed models of GDP, you see what makes up each part of the calculation. Taxes are seen in two parts of the equation. You obviously see taxes represented under government spending because government spending is dependent on taxes. But the amount of taxes used for government spending comes out of consumption spending. That means that government spending comes at the expense of private consumption spending. And this proves my earlier point that the government doesn't create anything; it simply redistributes resources. When government officials say that they created something, that's a lie. They collectively stole money from productive people in our society and spent it on government programs.

The United States has spent over $22 trillion on the War on Poverty since 1964.[3] The war on poverty was declared despite the United States poverty rates declining sharply and consistently since 1950. In 1950, the poverty rate was well above 30%. In 1963, the year before the war on poverty, the poverty rate was 19.5%. The downward trend continued until 1973. In 1973, the poverty rate was 11.1%. Since 1973, the poverty rate in the United States has continued to rise and fall between 10% to 15%. The highest poverty rates were seen in 1983 (15.2%), 1993 (15.1%), and 2010 (15.1%). The lowest rates were seen in 1973 (11.1%) and 2019 (10.5%).[4]

Spending on entitlement programs has continued to rise since LBJ's War on Poverty. In 2020, Medicaid cost $680 billion; Temporary Assistance for Needy Families (TANF) spent roughly $29 billion; and Supplemental Nutrition Assistance Program (SNAP) spent $79 billion[6]. These three programs cost more than $750 billion in one year. You would think that with the billions of dollars annually thrown at poverty, we would begin to solve the problem. Or at the very least, have more consistency in the poverty rates. But no. Government officials want to keep buying votes with the delusion that giving people money will end poverty. Ronald Reagan was right when he said, "Some years ago, the federal government declared war on poverty, and poverty won."

There is another problem. The GDP model does not account for deficit spending. Deficit spending is when the U.S. government spends more money than it earns in tax revenue. Deficits can increase and decrease year to year; if the government runs a yearly deficit, it is added to the total debt. Governments typically pay off the national debt by having more tax revenue than expenses (budget surplus). The United States has engaged in deficit spending for over twenty years. The last budget surplus was in 2001. In the early 2000s, the deficit spending was fairly low (relative to today's standards). This was during George W. Bush's presidency. The highest annual deficit that George W. Bush accrued was in 2008, when he accrued a budget deficit of $450 billion. George W. Bush's presidency on average, accrued roughly $248 billion annually from 2001 to 2009.[8]

The deficit would increase under Obama's first presidential term. In 2009, the national budget deficit was $1.42 trillion. Throughout Obama's first presidential term, he would average budget deficits over $1 trillion per year.

In his second presidential term, Obama's deficit spending declined. The lowest point of deficit spending was in 2015 when deficit spending was at $410 billion. The deficit then climbed in 2015 to $590 billion. Obama accrued an average of roughly $910 billion from 2009 to 2016.

And this is not a Democrat vs. Republican issue. Donald Trump did not stop the deficit spending. He increased the annual deficit spending every year of his presidency. Donald Trump accrued $670 billion deficit in 2017; $780 billion deficit in 2018; $980 billion deficit in 2019; and $3.13 deficit trillion in 2020. The massive jump in 2020 was due to the COVID-19 pandemic and the response from the government. But even without the COVID-19 pandemic, Trump's deficit spending likely would have exceeded $1 trillion in 2020.

I am talking about these presidents' deficit spending to show that this is something that everyone is engaging in. Democrats may have exacerbated the spending in the late 2000s. But Republicans have shown little to no interest in stopping the spending. Two problems arise out of these massive deficit spending habits.

I said earlier that GDP models do not account for deficit spending. Those models assume that the annual budgets are balanced. When the United States engages in deficit spending, it will skew the GDP model. The taxes taken away from consumption spending will equal the amount of taxes available for government spending in a GDP model with a balanced budget. This is not the case with deficit spending.

The taxes that are taken out of consumption spending will be less than the amount of taxes available for government spending in a GDP model with a budget deficit. You will see a false increase in GDP due to the amount of government spending. This means that the economy may not be performing as well as it seems.

One of the highlights of the Trump presidency was the "booming" economy. But how strong would the economy have been if Trump were not averaging $810 billion in deficit spending from 2017 to 2019?[5] Note: I am excluding economic data for 2020 because the COVID-19 pandemic was a massive externality that threw the entire U.S. economy out of balance. In the first quarter of 2017, the U.S. GDP was $19.148 trillion. In the fourth quarter of 2019, the U.S. GDP was $21.706 trillion. Over three years the GDP grew approximately $2.558 trillion. In that same timeframe, the United States accrued $2.43 trillion in government debt. That means that the United States economy barely outgrew its debt and that a substantial portion of U.S. GDP growth can be attributed to deficit spending.

And the deficit spending continued after Donald Trump left office. Joe Biden continued the trend. In 2021, despite having COVID-19 vaccines, the United States ran a $2.7 trillion deficit. In 2022, the United States ran a $900 billion deficit. In 2023, Joe Biden suggested a $6.8 trillion budget; if the United States brought in the same amount of tax revenue it did in 2022, this would cause a yearly deficit of nearly $2 trillion in 2023.

This imbalance can cause a false sense of economic security. And the money owed from deficit spending does not go away. Those debts accrue over time and accumulate to make up our national debt. That brings me to the worst problem the United States Government has created to date.

To attract investors, U.S. Treasury bonds must accrue interest. And when you have a high base amount of debt, you will have high interest payments, even if the interest rates are low. In 2021, The United States paid $413 billion in interest payments on our debt. The United States took in just over $4 trillion in tax revenue in 2021. Nearly 10% of U.S. revenue went toward the interest payments on our debt. And we did not even begin to repay it. The U.S. government decided to continue the trend of running budget deficits and added another $2.7 trillion to our national debt. As of March 1, 2023, the United States' national debt is over $31 trillion.[6] Even with interest rates between 1 and 2% per year, the United States will pay between $300 billion to $600 billion every year in interest alone. And with a national debt of over $30 trillion, the United States faces a very long payment process.

Let me show you what this scenario would look like from the viewpoint of your average American in a similar situation. I'm going to try to keep things simple in this example. So, the numbers may not be 100% on point with a real-life situation. This is just for demonstrative purposes.

Let's say you have an American who makes $50,000 a year but has amassed $375,000 in credit card debt. In this scenario, the interest rate on the credit card is a low flat rate of 1.5% and the American only makes one payment a year. The American will pay $5,625 in interest payments during the first year of the debt: That's 11.25% of the American's annual income paid only on the interest. This person will still have to pay rent, insurance, food, car payments, and other living expenses as well as payments on the total amount owed on the debt. Let's say this person only spends 70% of their income on living expenses ($35,000) and all their excess income goes toward paying the loan. The person will pay $15,000 a year until the debt is relieved. Interest payments are included in the $15,000 payment. If the person pays 30% of their revenue, it will take 31.5 years to repay the loan. And by the time the loan is paid, the borrower would have paid $98,519 in interest. The total cost of the loan will have jumped from $375,000 to $473,519.

It's too bad that American politicians do not understand the concept of compound interest because they continue to borrow money and inflate the debt. I would argue that many politicians in Washington, DC believe that we can continue to borrow money ad infinitum. That means they have no desire to repay the debts of people they are borrowing from. I would like to say congratulations to these idiot politicians. They just ruined our future and created (at least to my knowledge) the first publicly held Ponzi scheme. A word of advice: If you are looking to invest your money, do not invest in long-term government bonds. Like all Ponzi schemes, the final round of investors/suckers lose their money.

I know what you're thinking. "Well China holds all of our debt, so why should I be worried if the United States can't pay back its loans to them." In 2021, roughly 33% of the United States debt is held by foreign investors. At the end of 2022, the publicly held debt was roughly $24 trillion. I don't know how high the national debt needs to be before investors stop buying American bonds. Greece defaulted on its debt when its debt to GDP ratio was 180%. In June of 2021, the American debt to GDP ratio was at 125%. If America defaulted today, you are looking at a minimum of $16 trillion in wealth loss in the economy. For reference, U.S. households lost $19.2 trillion during the 2008 financial crisis.[7]

This time it would be worse. During the Great Recession, the Federal Reserve was able to use quantitative easing to help the economy recover. Quantitative easing is when the Federal Reserve purchases securities from banks. This is so that banks can lend that money to consumers. The Federal Reserve will also lower interest rates to stimulate demand for investment. All this is done to drive investment and productivity. The Obama administration also spent hundreds of billions of dollars on economic stimulus and bank bailouts. The bank bailouts were used to address the toxic assets on the banks' balance sheets. Toxic assets are investments that have lost their value and cannot be sold, making them worthless. The toxic assets during the great recessions were caused by securities from subprime mortgages.

In this case of a government default, the toxic assets would be U.S. Treasury bonds. Seeing the potential collapse, consumers would try to get money out of their bank accounts, causing bank runs. Banks and other financial institutions would face collapse due to the toxic assets that have flooded the market. Americans would try to liquidate their assets and limit their losses. The stock market would likely crash. This will lead to a recession and likely an economic depression.

The U.S. government would lose all financial credibility. However, this time the United States government would not be able to do any sort of intervention because the government would not have any money. And the government would not be able to find investors to buy bonds because of the recent default. The United States would likely still be in a budget deficit, so severe cuts would have to be made. The cuts will likely be directed toward entitlement programs and defense spending. And this is assuming that the government default happened today.

The U.S. government continues to accumulate debt. The congressional budget office projects that in 2033, the amount of debt held by the public will be $46.445 trillion.[9] And the net interest paid that year will be over $1.4 trillion. Even if we don't fiscally collapse during that time, the crushing weight of the debt will cause massive economic stagnation.

So, after you read this book, please call your local congressman, and thank them properly for destroying any future our economy might have had.

Family/Marriage

The family unit has been a key institution throughout history. From a biological perspective, parents have the greatest interest in the well-being of their children. And it does not take a village to raise a child. All it takes is a family with two parents who work together to provide and care for their children. Parents are not perfect (more on that later), but they are the most invested party in the safety and well-being of their children. After all, the passing down and survival of one's genes is a basic biological desire that exists in all species. Marriage is a key institution for the family unit. Simply put, marriage is a contract between (at least traditionally) a man and a woman. The man will abandon his sexual liberty and agree to stay with one woman. The typical male role is to provide resources and protect the family. The woman will abandon her hypergamous pursuits and stay with the man, traditionally taking on a support role with childcare being one of her main duties. The two will work with the primary goal of creating a stable environment for the next generation.

The collapse of the nuclear family has become increasingly evident in recent decades. According to Pew Research, the number of single mothers in the United States has risen dramatically from 1960 to 2011. In 1960, single motherhood was less than 10% of all households; today it exceeds 20%. The reasons for single motherhood have also changed. In 1960, only 4% of single mothers had never married; in 2011, women who had never married made up 44% of single mothers. That's an increase by a factor of eleven, and that's not counting for the overall increase in single mothers[11]. This demonstrates one of the biggest breakdowns in the family unit.

Marriage rates are also on the decline. According to the CDC, in populations of a thousand people, the marriage rate was 10.6% in 1980. The rate in 2018 was 6.5%.[12]

There are several reasons for the decline in marriage. Millennials and Gen Z saw a lot of divorces and are probably reluctant to continue the cycle. Another reason is that there are misconceptions about what marriage is and what it should be based on.

In the first paragraph, did I say anything about love? No, I didn't. Whoever came up with the idea that "marriage is about love" deserves a kick in the ass. The purpose of marriage is not to love one another but to create a stable family unit for raising the next generation. It is important for the two people to have chemistry and maintain unit cohesion. But love is not at the foundation of marriage. It is rare for a couple to still love each other the same way after ten years. In many cases love dies.

For that reason, it is naive to consider love as the foundation of marriage. Duty is at the foundation of marriage. The duty to the new family unit becomes more important than personal desires. Because you are no longer simply responsible for yourself; people depend on you. And failure impacts them as well.

Some people find happiness in marital bliss, but personal happiness is a secondary objective. Ensuring the next generation is given a stable environment is the number one priority.

The second thing you should notice is the roles. In the modern era, gender roles have become somewhat controversial. Some people favor traditional masculine and feminine roles in the family unit: The man provides the resources, and the wife supports him. Daddy paints the barn. Mama bakes the bread. But there are others who would like to see the roles change in some way. Typically, this change involves the woman providing resources for the family as well. While I personally favor the more traditional approach, it doesn't have to be that way for everybody. Different strokes for different folks.

But it is important that the roles are well-defined and that both parties bring value to the unit.

There are many metaphors for marriage. One that I heard of is that marriage is like two people dancing. Dancing requires a leader and a follower, and when the two dancers are in conflict, they fail at dancing. But I figured I'd give you a bizarre example. Marriage is like army infantry squads.

It may seem strange to compare army infantry squads to marriages. Why bring up the military? Because the army is exceptional at creating cohesive units with defined roles that achieve difficult goals. This can be seen in an army infantry squad. Two types of infantrymen are the rifleman and the machine gunner. The machine gunners and riflemen complement one another, providing strength where the other is weak. If the squad is attacked, it is the job of the machine gunner to keep a sustained barrage of bullets on the enemy's area. This is because a machine gun is designed for rapid firing, and it has a large ammo capacity. The rifleman's job is to fire accurately and precisely to protect the machine gunner and the flank. Rifles such as the M4 are designed to be precise and accurate, even at ranges exceeding five hundred meters.

It doesn't necessarily matter who has a rifle and who has an MG. Infantry are trained in both. What matters is that both understand the roles they are designed to play. A machine gunner cannot fulfill the role of someone with a rifle. An MG is not designed to have that level of accuracy and precision; it is designed for area targeting. An army machine gunner once told me that his job is to put a wall of lead between the squad and the enemy. And a rifleman can't do the job of a machine gunner. While the rifle is more accurate and precise, if you fire an M4A1 on full automatic, it will run out of ammo in a couple of seconds. The two must work together and complement each other.

I also said that both parties must bring value. Meaning that one party can't drop their gun and run away. If the machine gunner drops his gun and runs away, the rifleman will be overwhelmed. If the rifleman runs away, then the machine gunner will be flanked by the enemy.

It's the same concept in marriage. People must take either the role of leader or supporter. If a woman wants to take charge of the household and be the breadwinner, that's a necessary discussion for the family.

The reason a traditional marital arrangement works best is because there is a correlation between women earning more money than their husbands and marital dissatisfaction. According to a study by the University of Chicago, "A married woman earning more increases the probability of unhappiness in her union. Using data from 4,000 married couples surveyed as part of the U.S. National Survey of Families and Households, the researchers show that the percentage of people who report being "very happy" with their marriage declines when a woman earns more money than her husband. While close to 50% of wives and husbands report being very happily married, both spouses are 6 percentage points less likely to report a "very happy" marriage when the wife earns more. They're 8 percentage points more likely to report marital troubles in the past year and 6 percentage points more likely to have discussed separating in the past year. A woman outearning her husband could even doom the marriage as the researchers report this "increases the likelihood of divorce by 50%."[56] When one party decides to walk away, the entire unit will face the repercussions of the divorce, including but not limited to financial ruin and poverty.

Before I end this section, I want to mention something. If you don't want children, do not get married. If you are a guy, get a vasectomy. You can still have long-term relationships, but the primary reason for getting married does not exist if you do not want kids. To be clear, I am not saying that people who don't want kids should not be allowed to get married. In the United States, marriage has been seen as a right for everyone since the Obergefell Supreme Court decision in 2015. But doing something doesn't necessarily mean that you should do it. Be honest with your significant other about not wanting kids so that you do not waste the woman's time. And if she doesn't want kids either, then the two of you can look at a long-term relationship.

If you do not plan to have kids, any benefits in modern marriages can also be had outside of marriage. In this scenario, marriage for men is an all-risk no-reward scenario. And the risks can be the difference between life and death for some. A study by the University of California, Riverside showed "higher risks of suicide were found in divorced than in married persons. Divorced and separated persons were over twice as likely to commit suicide as married persons... Being single or widowed had no significant effect on suicide risk. When data were stratified by sex, it was observed that the risk of suicide among divorced men was over twice that of married men... Among women, however, there were no statistically significant differentials in the risk of suicide by marital status categories."[57]

If you're looking only for companionship, just stay in a committed, long-term relationship without getting married. Believe it or not, people have premarital sex. And without the safety net of marriage, the man and woman will have to remain at their best because their relationship is unsecured. You can even cohabitate with your significant other if you want to do that. Although I suggest looking at your state's cohabitation laws before you do this.

Remember, marriage is for raising the next generation. If you do not plan to have kids, there is no reason for marriage. The entire purpose of marriage is to create a stable and safe environment for the next generation. Where does this idea come from? It comes from evolutionary psychology.

One of the biological desires in nearly all species is to pass down one's genetic material. There is a way to ensure a legacy, even though life is finite. In most animals, the male will mate with a female and leave the female to care for the offspring. The male's biological strategy is to mate with as many females as possible so that the male's genetic legacy spreads far and wide. The female strategy is to mate with what females consider a high-quality partner, so that superior genes are passed down to their offspring.

Take cats for example. Our feline overlords are not only capable of spreading to every corner of the Internet, but to many climates and ecosystems. When a female cat is in heat, she will attract a male cat and mate with it. Once the females heat cycle ends, the male leaves. The female's pregnancy will last for approximately two months. Once the litter of kittens is born, the mother cat will provide for them. After eight to twelve weeks, the kittens will be independent and ready to live on their own.

But humans and cats are not the same. While humans and cats share a similar biological drive, only humans have adopted the concept of marriage. The reason for the difference comes from the developmental stages for humans. Humans have a very slow growth and development cycle. While babies are adorable, they have a high level of dependence that lasts for years. As Stewie Griffin from *Family Guy* said, "We're one! Independence means we die!"

Even during pregnancy that can last more than nine months, women face physical difficulties that put them and the child at risk. And after the child is born, without a man to provide, the mother will have to provide resources for herself and her child, while caring for the child and dealing with the physical aftermath of pregnancy.

Marriage in its earliest form, came from realizing the extreme risks of leaving women alone during and after pregnancy. As a result, men decided to stay and provide for the women they impregnated. It wasn't a purely altruistic idea; it was a logical solution to ensure the survival of their offspring.

Say a man follows the role of a cat and impregnates many women over the course of his life and leaves when the woman is pregnant. It may seem like he has fulfilled his biological desire to pass on his genes. But what good does that do if most or all the children die young because the mother could not simultaneously care for the children and provide the resources they needed?

So, men had an idea: Instead of having kids with many partners and leaving, they would commit to one woman and have multiple kids with her. The man would work to provide resources and protection for the woman and kids. Women would watch and care for the kids. This allowed favorable outcomes for both parties. Women would have some parental pressures alleviated, allowing for a greater chance that the kids will survive. Rather than having many children with slim chances of survival, men would have multiple children with moderate chances of the children living to adulthood.

This was marriage in its earliest form. Over time, marriage was influenced by religion, politics, and the Hallmark Channel. But the core reason for getting married is to raise the next generation. It is a pointless and unnecessary risk to create a family unit of two people.

Education

My opinion of the government isn't the only thing that has changed over the last decade. I used to think that the education system was sufficient. This is mostly because I went to a decent public school (at least by rural Louisiana and Kansas standards). There were a fair number of clubs, sports, and extracurricular activities. The curriculum was by the book, but teachers were allowed enough room for creative ways to teach. The teachers were also more concerned with teaching than being your friend. I'll talk about how this has changed in a later chapter.

After high school, I attended an eighteen-month program at Fortis College in Baton Rouge to become a medical laboratory technician (MLT). It wasn't the best experience. The school faced staffing issues during one of my semesters. As a result, I didn't have a teacher during most of my microbiology course, and I think microbiology counted for about 20% of the American Society of Clinical Pathology certification exam. But I was able to pass my certification and could then start working in the medical field. But after a year or two, I decided that I didn't care for the medical field.

I decided to go back to school to study economics while I worked as a full time MLT. I had to do four years of school because none of my previous credits would transfer. I started at Baton Rouge Community College, and after two years, I transferred to LSU. I graduated from LSU in May of 2019 with a bachelor's degree in economics.

The six years of school cost about $50,000 in student loans, which isn't that bad for six years of school. It helped that I didn't stay on campus. I also paid for books with my own money up front and not with loans. And not going to LSU all four years saved me over $15,000. Since then, my schooling allowed the opportunity to earn a six-figure salary; so, my school experience was an overall success.

If my story is a success, why do I consider the education system to be failing? It is because I see a lot of inefficiencies in the process of getting my education. And these inefficiencies were driven by and protected by teachers' unions and public policy.

I remember an old cartoon where a kid was asking why he had to go to school. He was told, "If you don't go to school, you go to jail." As he walked away, the child muttered, "School . . . jail . . . same thing."

That comic was not that inaccurate. Most kids are sentenced to thirteen years of primary education, and some students may have extended sentences for poor performance, which leads me to the first problem with the education system: Thirteen years is too long.

In economics, there is a concept called "diminishing returns." Diminishing returns show that as you increase time and/or resources on a project, the marginal output will decrease over time. The highest level of marginal output will be after the initial investment. But over time, the output will increase at a smaller and smaller rate. There will be a point where the opportunity cost of the investment will exceed the returns on your investment. This means that the time and resources that you are spending at that point would be better used somewhere else.

How does this translate to the classroom? When I was in first grade, I learned how to read and write. That initial result was the biggest increase in skill because I went from illiteracy to basic literacy. And I would gradually improve every year. This continued until I was around fifteen or sixteen years old. By that point, any gains that I made were insignificant. I would say that the last two years of high school didn't offer much. And I think the same could be said for a lot of people. Ask yourself, "Was there really a huge gap in necessary knowledge from the end of your tenth grade year to the end of your twelfth grade year?" By the end of your sophomore year, you had already been in school for more than a decade. Did another two years make that much difference?

You may be thinking, "But Mike, those last two years helped prepare you for college." Well dear reader, you are correct. But do you know what would have been better than college prep? Allowing me to go to college when I was sixteen. Your first two years at college are mostly a review of what you should have learned in high school. I'd say that 95% of my college algebra course at Baton Rouge Community College was reviewing things that I already knew. I can say the same thing for my American history, English, and biology classes.

So, here's an idea. Offer a high school diploma at the end of the tenth grade. Save students two years of their youth and let them make their own way. Sure, I enjoyed reading Beowulf my senior year in high school, but was it something that I needed to know to succeed? Probably not.

And what about the people who don't want to go to college? Why do they need to spend unnecessary time in high school? Why not allow them to start working or find an apprenticeship? That way they can start building their future at sixteen rather than eighteen.

For these people there is greater loss in those two years because what they learn doesn't serve a purpose in their lives. They should already be literate and have the basic mathematical skills necessary to enter the workforce. At that point, any marginal gains made in education are less than the marginal gains in workforce experience, especially if the student can receive a high school diploma.

The problem is that there will never be significant reforms to public education. If we allowed students to graduate high school at sixteen rather than eighteen, you would see teachers getting laid off. And that is something that the teachers' unions would not stand for. After all, students exist to serve the whims and special interests of teachers' unions. It is why teachers oppose school choice and are thereby willing to force students to attend failing public schools.

School choice is a program that allows students to have several education options available. Parents who may be limited in their options send their kids to public schools. But public education can be a boom or a bust. And states that do not allow for school choice make it mandatory for students to attend public schools in their assigned district. And if the school is low performing, parents cannot opt to send their kids to a different public school. In one incident a woman named Kelley Williams-Bolar tried to send her daughters to a better-performing school district in Akron, Ohio. When this was discovered by local authorities, she was arrested. She was sentenced to ten days in jail, eighty hours of community service, and three years' probation.[58]

It's tragic to see a parent being punished for the "crime" of caring about her daughter's education. If teachers' unions had their way, it would be like this everywhere. Without school choice, teachers' unions maintain a guaranteed monopoly with failing public schools. And you're lucky that teachers' unions even grant you that much.

During the COVID-19 pandemic, teachers' unions across the country fought to keep public schools shut down.[59] And in some cases, teachers' unions pushed for demands that had nothing to do with COVID-19. This can be seen by what a Los Angeles teachers' union demanded in June of 2020. The union demanded Medicare for all, raising state taxes, defunding the police and imposing moratoriums on charter schools[59].

Teachers' unions are always threatening to strike over teacher compensation. These unions demand that these glorified babysitters be paid more money. The fact that they only work about eight months out of the year is irrelevant. I remember that my high school gave two weeks off for Christmas, one week off for Easter, a week for Thanksgiving, and three months for summer break. This isn't counting Mardi Gras and other federal holidays. So, any time I hear a teacher complaining about their $40,000-a-year salary, I don't take it seriously because they have a lot more time for leisure than most people who work full time.

And it won't change because of the transparently corrupt collective bargaining in the U.S. Teachers' unions. They will support certain candidates running for office. Unions will donate funds and get their members to vote for candidates. In 2022, teachers donated 6.8 million dollars to Democrat politicians; compare that to the $26,000 dollars Republicans got from teachers' unions.[60] When those candidates take office, they will give better deals to these unions and essentially, act as a pretorian guard for the union. They oppose charter schools, school choice, and any significant reform that could harm these unions.

There are flaws in our public education system, and it's likely not going to change because of these unions, but I would argue that primary education with all its flaws isn't as bad as higher education. Sure, primary education can waste your time. But higher education suffers from the same inefficiencies and can waste your time, your money, and destroy your future.

The inefficiency I saw when I was in high school multiplied when I was in higher education. In one of my management courses, my professor asked students about our degrees. This management course was required for all business degrees, but he asked us about some other required courses. He asked why we had to take courses that were irrelevant to our degree. Why did Econ majors have to take Intro to Fiction? Why did STEM majors have to take speech courses? Hell, even my editor said that he had to take biology courses for his English degree! The typical explanation from the students was, "Well it makes us more well-rounded." Our idealism was adorable. The real reason for our taking these courses was so that schools could milk us for thousands of extra dollars. In my case, I took courses such as Intro to Fiction,

Intro to Fine Arts, several speech courses, two biology courses, and five free electives at LSU. If I had not been forced to take these courses, I probably would have saved around $10,000 in tuition, at least $1,000 in books, and one year of my time.

This is why taking unnecessary courses is more detrimental in higher education than it is in primary education. In higher education, you must pay for these courses. Standards for degrees should be changed to better fit each degree. There should be less required hours. This means the unnecessary or irrelevant classes would be cut from our schedules. Think about it. No calculus for art majors. No political science classes for STEM fields. No "check your cisgendered white male privilege" class for anyone!

But this won't happen because colleges would lose money. Colleges do not care about students or their future. If they did, they would not make students waste years and thousands of dollars on electives that they do not need. A good example of colleges not caring about the students' future is when "THE" Ohio State University hosted a seminar promoting OnlyFans for students. For those who don't know, OnlyFans is a subscription-based content creation platform. Over the last couple of years, it has become most known for women posting revealing photos of themselves for money. If you ever hear a woman say, "I am a content creator for OnlyFans," that's code for "I do amateur pornography." Nothing says, "I care about my students' future and credibility" more than promoting amateur pornography platforms at your university.

One way students destroy their future is by going to college to have the "college experience." The "college experience" is a meme that needs to die. It is idiotic to spend tens of thousands of dollars so you can drink and party with a bunch of dude bros. You may have been able to get away with that in the past, but it's too expensive to do that today. In 1989–1990, the average annual cost of tuition to attend a four-year public university was $1,780. Adjusted for inflation (by 2020 standards), the cost would be $3,605. But the average cost at a public, four-year university was $9,345 in 2019-2020[61]. The point is, if you want to drink with friends, go to a bar or a club. You are treating what is supposed to be a key investment as if it is a consumable good or service. And you do not get any ROI (return on investment) from consuming things.

Going for the "college experience" is often accompanied by getting a useless degree. I would define a useless degree as "a college education that has a cost (in both time and money) that exceeds the benefit or return on the investment." You do not need to earn a six-figure salary to show you obtained a useful degree (although that wouldn't hurt). Let's suppose one man can cut some of his college costs by working during school. He graduates from college with $25,000 in student loans. He can find a job that pays around $50,000 a year. Without the degree, he would have found a job paying only $40,000 a year. So, he incurs a yearly benefit of $10,000 that would not be available without his degree. After roughly three years, the degree will exceed the $25,000 cost. The yearly benefit is more than $20,000 of yearly spending. This means the degree was beneficial to him.

Unfortunately, useless degrees are another common theme with higher education. Students will take on tens of thousands, and in some cases over $100,000 in student loan debt for a degree that does nothing for them income wise. I heard this simple rule of thumb when it comes to student debt. The amount of money that you take out in student debt should be less than or equal to one year's salary for your projected career field. So, if you have a projected career that pays $50,000 a year, do not take on more than $50,000 in debt.

Unfortunately, a lot of people do not take this advice. I recall a story where a young woman took out $100,000 in student loans for a drama degree. That is a huge amount to take out on education. Even with low interest rates, she can expect to pay at least $4000 a year in interest payments alone. And what did she do once she graduated college? She started working as a receptionist and a production assistant. I believe she made around $40,000 a year. At that point, she had gained no benefit from her degree. Even if she paid $500 a month on her student loans, interest would take at least half of any progress she made on her loans. She wasted four years of her youth and dramatically hurt her financial stability. And she didn't expect to find success because she said that she routinely called her senator to ask about student loan forgiveness. Meaning she wanted a bailout from the American taxpayer because she chose a useless degree.

And this sort of story is not uncommon. Every now and then we'll hear people complaining about their student loan debt and how they have no way of paying it back. In 2022, Joe Biden tried to relieve $10,000 to $20,000 in student debt for people making less than $125,000 a year. Since he tried doing it through executive action without congressional approval, the courts stopped the relief.

There is a way to stop this awful trend. And no, it's not free college. The first rule of economics is that there is no such thing as "free." When you make something "free," you simply shift the cost from one party to another. Unless you expect teachers and administrators to work for free, colleges will still incur operating expenses. And with no revenue coming in from students, where does the money come from? Governmental entities is the probable answer. This means that free college will simply lead to the American taxpayer subsidizing the dude bro debt parties.

The government needs to stop giving public student loans and let the private sector handle this. The problem with public student loans is that they will give loans to nearly anybody. While this may seem good on paper, there are several negative effects of these loans.

The obvious problem is that these loans allow people who should not be getting loans to borrow money; at the very least there should be a limit on how much students are allowed to borrow. The receptionist who took out $100,000 for a drama degree is an example of this. She has crippled herself financially.

In the current situation, no one is going to do a cost benefit analysis on the loans. It is almost like the subprime mortgage loans that caused the Great Recession. In the subprime mortgage fiasco, people with "no jobs, no assets" were able to take out loans for hundreds of thousands of dollars. And because these people had no way of paying off these loans, they defaulted and destroyed their credit. The same negligence that caused the great recession is causing the current student loan crisis.

The school doesn't care if you will be unable to pay back your loans. They are already getting their money although they might ask you for donations after you graduate. The government doesn't care about your ability to repay the loans. They are going to get paid one way or another. Declaring bankruptcy does not get rid of public student loans. And if you default on your loans, the government should withhold any income tax refund until your debt is cleared.

Private lenders will take more into consideration when it comes to lending because they lose money if you don't repay the loan. It doesn't matter what type of loan it is as long as the loan is not sponsored or influenced by the government. The lender will do everything they can to ensure the loan is repaid. For college students, this will likely include an analysis of the borrower's projected future income, credit score, the desired major, GPA, and the requested loan amount will be taken into consideration. It might take a few years, but worthless degrees will become endangered if not extinct. Note: for more knowledge on useless degrees, read *Worthless* by Aaron Clarey).

I am not saying that liberal arts degrees should be banned or that people should not be allowed to get degrees of their choosing. In America, you have the right to be the author of your own story and chase your dreams. However, you are not entitled to chase your dreams at the expense of others. Other people should not be forced to pay for your mistakes. In other words, no student loan bailouts for $100,000-useless degrees. There is nothing wrong with ensuring people who take out loans repay their debts. And there is nothing compassionate about giving people loans that cannot be paid back.

Another problem with these public loans is that their limitless availability to everyone raises the price of tuition. A rule in economics is that if you increase demand for a good or service and keep everything else the same, you will see an increase in price. By allowing everyone access to higher education, demand has exponentially increased while supply cannot keep up. As a result, we have seen a massive increase in the cost of tuition. According to *U.S. News & World Report,* over the last twenty years, "tuition and fees at private national universities have jumped 134%. Out-of-state tuition and fees at public national universities have risen 141%. In-state tuition and fees at public national universities have grown the most, increasing 175%." [13]

And there are alternatives to taking out massive public student loans. For starters, you can cut the cost of the first two years of your education in half by going to a community college instead of a major university. The tuition cost for a full-time student at Baton Rouge Community College was roughly

$2000 per semester in 2017. In that same period, it cost more than $6000 for a full-time semester at LSU in 2017. And in 2017-2018 Tulane University in New Orleans had a tuition cost of $24,460 per semester.[62] Accredited junior colleges can save parents tens of thousands of dollars in tuition expenses over the course of any loans. The 4% interest on a $20,000 loan is a lot more manageable than 4% on a $100,000 loan.

And there are alternatives to private loans. In some states public scholarship programs are available. For example, Louisiana has the Taylor Opportunity Program for Students (TOPS). The merit-based, state-funded scholarship program is available to Louisiana residents. The scholarship is only available for approved Louisiana-based schools and universities. Typical requirements for TOPS include taking the ACT and having minimum GPA requirements. Scholarship amounts differ among schools. In 2022, TOPS paid $3,731.49 for a semester at LSU and $1,543.04 at Baton Rouge Community College.[63] Regardless of my opinion on TOPS and similar programs, if these programs are available in your state, it is wise to take advantage of them. If the state is going to spend money, then it might as well benefit you.

Another possibility is income share agreements (ISA). An ISA is technically considered a student loan, but it is different than traditional loans. Traditional loans charge you the amount borrowed with interest. You are expected to make payments until the entire balance is paid off regardless of your employment status or prospects. An ISA works differently.

Instead of having an entire set balance to pay off, you agree to pay a percentage of your income over a set period. The percentage of your salary that you agreed to repay is called the *income share percentage*; the length of time is called the *repayment period*. The income share percentage varies on a case-to-case basis. And the repayment period usually lasts somewhere between two and ten years.

There is also a salary floor. A salary floor is the minimum amount your salary needs to be in order for payments to be collected. If your salary floor is greater than your income, payments will not be collected. Some ISAs even allow these periods to count against your repayment period. This can offer more flexibility and guarantees. It is even possible for someone to pay less money than the amount borrowed.

Nerd wallet has a free calculator and information on ISAs; check it out at https://www.nerdwallet.com/article/loans/student-loans/income-share-agreements-what-students-should-know-before-borrowing.[64]

As with primary education, there will never be real reform. Instead of unions, you have politicians being incentivized to keep the system as it is. What would happen if Congress ended public student loan programs? You would get a bunch of students complaining that they are unable to finish their last couple years of school because they can't get funding for their degree in gender studies. Those students wouldn't realize that the government just saved them tens of thousands of dollars and years of their time. Politicians are unwilling and unable to handle the political fallout that comes with such changes.

And you would likely see something similar if politicians tried to reform degree requirements. Instead of angry students, there would be a bunch of angry university teachers and administrators. They wouldn't be happy that the school or university is going to lose thousands of dollars in revenue each year. Ten bucks says that they would accuse politicians of defunding universities at that point.

One of the rules of politics is, "Don't give your opponents a reason to vote for them instead of you." Any politician that would agree to end public student loans or change degree requirements would create an angry constituent base. The politician would be lucky to survive a primary election, let alone a general election. And voters would not like this change because it's easier to offer them ice cream than to convince them to eat broccoli,. So, it is in the politician's best interest to avoid rocking the boat. And any change to higher education is unlikely.

# Reason 3: Modern Parents Suck

"Your Parents love themselves more than they love you."

—Aaron Clarey

If you do not want kids, then take preventative means to avoid having them. Many forms of birth control are available. And while most of them are designed for women, new forms of non-hormonal male birth control are being developed. One of the biggest problems plaguing our society today is crappy parents. Proper parenting is a hard job. And if you're not willing to do it right, don't do it at all.

Many wonderful parents do the best they can to provide a stable environment for their kids. Sometimes the foster parents are amazing. Official and unofficial adoptive parents have made a huge impact on the lives of many children.

A coworker of mine, Dana, told me that she and her husband had taken in more than a few kids who had essentially been abandoned by their parents. In one instance, a mother abandoned her teenager so she could go and spend time with her new boyfriend. The dad wasn't living in the state at the time, so he had no idea what was going on. The mom left her kid alone with no food, money, or other provisions. Fortunately, Dana and her husband were quite charitable. They showed the kind of generosity that must have been strenuous. But it made all the difference in the world for the kids they helped.

Some of the best parents a person could have are not their biological parents. I had a similar story with Helen Christine Palmer. I called her Aunt Chris, but she was more of an adoptive mother to me. My mom passed when I was young. Aunt Chris was a very loving and wonderful person. When I was little, I remember that she would sing me to sleep. When I cried, she would support me. I tried to look after her when she was older.

Fortunately, her two children (my older adoptive siblings) did a good job of helping her. Tim, Amanda, and I loved her dearly. When she died in 2022, it left a hole in our hearts. And the world will never be the same. That's how I know she was a great parent to me. While I would not say that our time together was cut short, I selfishly wish that we could have had a little more time together.

If you had genuinely good parents, you should be very happy with that experience. You need to call or visit your parents regularly. They likely kept you as safe as they could from the horrors of the world. But they also didn't coddle you, and they created an adult child as a result. That's not an easy balance to strike. My rule is if they were good to you when you were young, you need to be good to them when they are old.

Unfortunately, many people today do not have such luck. That's why this chapter will appeal to a lot of people. Parents have failed their children in many ways. Many people have been subjected to abuse in one way or another due to the actions of bad parents. But it doesn't always have to end in abuse. It is common today for a child's parents to get divorced and ruin the sense of security that came with a functional family unit.

In this chapter, I am going to discuss four archetypes of bad parents. I'm sure that you could find more if you wanted. I am simply going with the four that seem most prevalent and damaging.

The Deadbeat Dad

This is one that needs no introduction. The deadbeat dad is a man who abandons all personal responsibility for his children. He had no intention of getting a woman pregnant but most likely decided not to use any form of protection. Because, you know, actions never have consequences.

The deadbeat dad is probably the most common type of parent in this chapter. Chapter 2 mentions the rise in single motherhood. The deadbeat dad is at least half responsible for that rise.

Like all the types of parents listed in this chapter, this type is unworthy of anyone's respect. Even less can be said of their personal intelligence. These guys probably turned a one-night stand into an eighteen-year financial commitment because they don't like condoms. And if you don't pay your child support, you're going to jail.

I knew a guy who got a girl pregnant when he was young. And he got hit hard with child support. He went to jail several times because he was behind on his payments. And he still had to pay child support, even though he was in jail.

There is a weird game that courts play. The courts demand someone pay child support and send them to jail if they fall behind. And then the courts get mad because the guy can't make money while in jail. So once the guy gets out of jail, they send him back to jail because he made no money while he was in jail. If there is anything that needs reform, it's the family court.

So, after several years of being in and out of jail, the guy was able to get out of his child support obligation. This was because the ex-girlfriend got married and her new husband was willing to adopt the kid. So, he was free from his obligation.

He could now start to rebuild his life. After all, he was still young. I believe he was in his late twenties. He could now start to build his skills, control his finances, and take control of his life. It may not have been the most ideal situation, but a late start is better than no start.

So, what does he do with his newfound freedom and potential? He kept a job, stayed out of trouble, and was building a future. This lasted about a year or two. But because unprotected sex was such a great idea the first time, I guess he figured why not do it again? He got another girl pregnant. This time he didn't even try to pay child support. Or make any effort to see his kid. He pretty much laid low and prayed that he wouldn't run into any cops.

Here's the problem with these guys. It is not just their own lives that they are wrecking, but the lives of the kids as well. Children growing up without fathers is one of the worst things that can happen in our society. Below is a small list of problems that result from deadbeat dads.[14]

- "85% of youth who are currently in prison grew up in a fatherless home. (Texas Department of Corrections).
- Children without a father are four times more likely to be living in poverty than children with a father (*National Public Radio*).
- Children from fatherless homes are twice as likely to drop out of school before graduating than children who have a father in their lives (*National Public Radio*).
- Children who live in a single-parent home are more than twice as likely to commit suicide than children in a two-parent home (*The Lancet*).
- 85% of all children who exhibit some type of a behavioral disorder come from a fatherless home (U.S. Department of Justice).
- 90% of the youth in the United States who decide to run away from home, or become homeless for any reason, originally come from a fatherless home (U.S. Department of Justice)."[14]

In closing this section, there is one more thing to note. If you want to be a part of your kids' lives but haven't been able to see your kids for a long time, this chapter does not pertain to you. A close friend was put through the hell that is family court. Even facing bankruptcy, all he cared about was being able to see his kids. But the ex-wife had lied and brainwashed them into hating their father. I saw firsthand that these kids had come to hate their father. Even after all the things he had tried to do for them.

If this story rings true to you, you are likely a good man and a good father. Wanting to see your children is an admirable goal, and it's unfortunate you were dealt a terrible hand. May God bless you in any periods of darkness you face.

The "Snake-in-the-Garden" Parent

I'm sure most people know or are aware of the biblical story of Adam and Eve. They were living in the Garden of Eden. God commands them not to eat the forbidden fruit of the tree of knowledge, but Eve is eventually tempted by a serpent. She convinces Adam to eat the fruit with her. When God discovers what they have done, he expels Adam and Eve from the garden.

Now in this section, the parent is not the serpent. Rather, the parent is the one who allowed the serpent into the garden. The snake will be an abuser of some kind. The abuse can be physical, sexual, or emotional. It all depends on what type of snake you're dealing with. And either through negligence or indifference, the parent fails to protect the child. One example of this is when predators target single moms to have access to their children. By the time the mom notices something is wrong, the damage has been done. And some moms disbelieve the child or are unwilling to do anything about the abuse.

I said earlier that these sections would ring true for a lot of people. Well, this is the section my brothers and I can relate to and probably many readers will too.

Our father's third marriage was to a psychopath. A common expression for a woman like her is "she had more red flags than a Chinese Communist Parade." When Dad met her, she was an adulterer and a recovering alcoholic. She was so terrible that she didn't have custody of her own kids. Lucky them.

She was mentally unstable, and she had a short-fused temper. She even tried to kill herself at one point. It may seem cruel to say, but it would have been better if she had succeeded. If that had happened, we would've been spared years of her torment. Looking back at it now, I know why that snake was abusive. She hated herself, and she took it out on everyone else.

I remember one morning—I think I was eight or maybe nine. At this point, I was already several years into her abuse. She was angry about something and needed to let off some steam. Dad had left for work. So, anything was on the table. She went through the house looking for some reason to beat me and my brothers. Spoilers: She found a reason to beat all of us.

I don't remember what great crimes my brothers committed, but they were probably like mine. What was my great crime? There was a shirt on my floor, underneath my bed. I didn't even know it was there.

That's how I know she was simply looking for someone to hit. She went as far as looking under my bed to find a reason. Hell, I'd bet five bucks that she put it there. I didn't see her search my room.

It's also worth noting that at that time, a spanking was not done with a hand or a belt although, I do remember one time she hit me about ten times with a belt when I was six. Around this time, the "tool of discipline" was a wooden boat oar. Why Dad thought that was a good idea, I'll never know.

Before she took us to school, she put the three of us on the couch and called us up one at a time. We would kneel in front of the couch and get hit three times on the ass. I still remember my turn. On the last strike, she missed my ass and hit my lower back. I went to school with my legs shaking, and they didn't stop shaking until I was safe in class.

About two years before my father divorced her (I think she cheated on him), she lightened up a bit. The beatings stopped for the most part. I figured that my strategy of being as small and quiet as possible worked. But that wasn't the reason. After talking to my brother Mark and his wife about this years later, I discovered something. It wasn't my strategy that made a difference. Remember, if she wanted to hit me, she could find a reason. No, that snake's focus shifted from beating all three of us to sexually grooming my older brother.

He was in his teens at the time. The snake would ground my brother a lot so that he couldn't leave the house, which is a classic move of an abuser. Isolate the victim so you can get them away from support groups.

And there were other signs of grooming. She would make him massage her. She was jealous of his girlfriends. There was even one instance where she took the gum he was chewing out of his mouth, put it in her mouth and started chewing it. I'm sure there was more, but I didn't want to push the issue. He had been through enough.

I haven't seen that snake in over fifteen years. And it's a good thing that I haven't. After all, I'm not that scared little boy anymore. Even though the snake is gone, my brother and I still feel the effects.

My brother had a panic attack a few years ago. This was due to his wife watching one of the snake's favorite movies. I think the movie was *Coyote Ugly*. If I had to guess, seeing that movie brought my brother back to a traumatic point in his life, and he had trouble dealing with it. He definitely has PTSD (post-traumatic stress disorder) from it. He also feels bad that he could not protect me. Being the oldest, he feels it was his job to keep us safe, but I can usually cheer him up by saying that despite everything, I get nostalgic for the times I spent with him. I may not have been safe, but I was happy when I was with him.

As for me: Now that I am older, I carry my scars well, but there was a time when I felt ashamed that I allowed myself to be a victim of that snake. And even more ashamed that I couldn't help my brother. I wish I had loudly rebelled and pushed back. I could have taken the heat off everyone else. It might have meant more beatings, but I could have handled it. If nothing else, I would have made that snake's life's a little bit more difficult. That's one of the things I learned about being an adult. You only have so many minutes a day, so many calories of energy that you are willing to expend on something. And if I could have made that snake waste 5 to 10 minutes of her day, every day, I know that it would have made her miserable. Just a little more miserable than she already was.

This shows something. I don't know how much money Dad lost in his divorce, but the price that my brothers and I paid was higher. That's what happens when parents let a snake into the garden. The parents pay for it at some point, but the child will pay for it even more. To all the "snake-in-the-garden" parents out there, whatever you got out of the relationship, I hope it was worth it.

And I know I'm not alone in this. According to U.S. Department of Health and Human Services, "More than 15 million children in the United States live in homes in which domestic violence has happened at least once. These children are at greater risk for repeating the cycle as adults by entering into abusive relationships or becoming abusers themselves. For example, a boy who sees his mother being abused is ten times more likely to abuse his female partner as an adult. A girl who grows up in a home where her father abuses her mother is more than six times as likely to be sexually abused as a girl who grows up in a non-abusive home.

Children who witness or are victims of emotional, physical, or sexual abuse are at higher risk for health problems as adults. These can include mental health conditions, such as depression and anxiety. They may also include diabetes, obesity, heart disease, poor self-esteem, and other problems."[66]

The Poser Parent

One of my favorite movies is *The Departed*. There is a scene where Martin Sheen and Mark Wahlberg interview Leonardo DiCaprio for a job as a Massachusetts State Police officer. Sheen asks DiCaprio, "Do you want to be a cop, or do you want to appear to be a cop? It's an honest question. A lot of guys want to appear to be cops. Gun, badge, pretend they're on TV."

In this scene Sheen is warning DiCaprio about the dangers of being a real cop. For DiCaprio, to be a real cop, he's going to go undercover and work to take down the head of the Irish mob. The job is hard work and exceedingly dangerous.

*The Departed* is a good movie, but the aforementioned scene can apply to people who want to be parents. Do you want to be a parent? It's an honest question. A lot of people want to appear to be parents. They have the cheesy Christmas cards and the kid's life story plastered all over social media.

The people that only want to appear to be parents are what you might call "poser parents." They usually care about having the appearance of a perfect family, rather than having a functioning family unit. It's a mirage. It's like the Instagram model who takes photos of herself at a nice beach, but she is a deeply sad, unfulfilled person. She smiles for the photos, but they are miserable for the rest of the day. Then she goes back to her apartment and pops antidepressants like candy.

The poser parent would post videos and pictures of the perfect family day. The husband, wife, and kids are all smiling. They are happy; they're loving, they're . . . lying for the camera. The faux happiness is there for the rest of the world. The family's happiness doesn't matter. One of the best examples of a poser parent is from a particular Reddit post. It's from a husband, talking about the hell he and his kids endured.

He starts off by saying that on the outside, it looked like his family had the perfect life—images of which seemed perfect for social media sharing. It seemed to everyone he had the perfect marriage. And his wife was more than happy to display the perfect family on social media.

But behind closed doors, the husband and the kids were miserable. He is in therapy for depression. And his youngest child is in therapy for anxiety/depression. The wife consistently threatens to take away everything in court, including the kids, if he ever thinks of leaving. There is no love, kindness, or basic respect for the husband. He and the kids are accessories for photos. That's it.

The wife is obviously the 'poser' parent in this scenario. All that matters to her is the false appearance of a happy family, but the family has lost nearly all function and cohesion. And there's obviously abuse.

But it doesn't have to be only one parent. Both parents can be 'poser parents.' A good example of this is family vlogging channels. It's where parents film themselves and their kids in their daily activities. And every now and then, the parents will set up some cheesy, scripted scene. One group of poser parents even had their son give his phone number to a daughter of another group of poser parents. Both kids were around the age of three and had no idea what was going on. It was cringeworthy.

But family vloggers do have one thing over the average poser parent. Family vloggers have a much larger level of child exploitation. Sure, the average poser parents might post a lot of pictures on social media, but children on a family vlogging channel will have hundreds or even thousands of hours of their lives posted on social media. All of this is without their consent. And it's out there for the whole world to see. Children will have embarrassing or painful life events posted, and the child's privacy has been sold for clicks and advertising revenue, but I suppose that the child's loss is the poser parents gain.

The Munchausen-by-Proxy Parent

Munchausen Syndrome by Proxy: A mental illness and form of child abuse. The caretaker of a child either forces fake symptoms or causes real symptoms to make the child appear sick.

If you've watched *The Sixth Sense,* you may be familiar with this one. In the movie, the ghost of a sickly child who passed away has a message for her father. She contacts one of the main characters, a kid who can talk to the dead. The dead girl wanted to show her father a video that she made. At first, the video is a sort of play that she created with dolls, but partway through the video, she hears her mother coming to her room with food, so she puts her dolls away, but she doesn't have time to put away the camera. The mother enters the room not knowing that the camera is still recording. Before the mother serves her daughter's soup, she puts something in it. It was likely some form of disinfectant. The plot twist was that the child wasn't sick; she was being poisoned by her mother. This is an example of a Munchausen syndrome by proxy parent. A parent who is willing to cause physical or psychological harm to their child so that they can receive attention from others. In this instance, the mom was physically harming her daughter so that she could appear to have the role of a caretaker.

The "Munchausen by Proxy" parent has become more visible today due to social media. But not in the way that you would think. The form of abuse is not poisoning the child as mentioned above. At least, not at first. These parents will try to instill gender confusion among their children. This is typically done at an early age before a child has had a chance to discover his or herself.

What the abuser does is not complicated. For example, if a mother has a son and wants to instill gender confusion in their child, she may start treating her son as a female. An example of someone meeting my definition of a "Munchausen by Proxy" parent is Jeanette Jennings, the mother of Jazz Jennings.

Jazz Jennings is a transgender icon. Jazz was a born a boy, but Jazz claims that there were desires to be a girl around the age of three.

In a *Time* article, Jazz wrote, "When I was around 2 years old, I had what I now refer to as the Good Fairy dream. After a long morning of playing with Ari's dolls, dressing them up and staring enviously at the smooth area between their legs, I took a nap in my sister's bed. I had no idea that I was asleep—the world seemed crystal clear as a grown woman wearing a blue gown floated into the room.

She wasn't quite like the imaginary creatures you see in cartoons, but I knew instinctively that she was a fairy, thanks to her gossamer wings, the glowing light all around her, and the magic wand that suddenly appeared in her hand. Other than those fantasy details, she looked and acted like an adult, full of purpose and authority.

I don't remember her exact words, or even if she spoke out loud at all, but I knew why she was there. She promised to use her wand to "turn my penis into a vagina."[65]

You might notice something strange about this memory. That is an extremely vivid and detailed memory. Do you think that someone at the age of two could remember something like that in that kind of detail? Or is it more plausible that Jeanette Jennings told Jazz that story many times and implanted a false memory?

It is not hard for someone to manipulate a small child. This can be done by putting the child in dresses and positively reinforcing the behavior. Even something as simple as praise and admiration makes an effective feedback loop for the child. This is because the child seeks the approval of the parent.

And the parent is more than happy to show off their new gender-confused child on social media. All the while they are using the child as a prop for their virtue signaling. Jeanette Jennings got more than most Munchausen by Proxy parents. She was able to get a reality TV show featuring Jazz (*I Am Jazz*) to air in 2015. A reality show that Jeanette conveniently has a part in the show which was still going in 2023.

Why is this harmful? If the parent is successful in convincing the child that he or she is transgender, this puts the child at a higher risk for mental illness and suicide. The elevated risk of suicide alone shows how selfish and irresponsible these parents are.

But that's just the mental harm the child can endure. Today children are given "puberty blockers." The idea is that these blockers can pause a child's puberty while the child thinks about what they want to do next. The concept of interrupting a child's development is wrong in and of itself. It's even worse when the medicine used to block their puberty is also used to chemically castrate sex offenders. For a more in-depth look at this subject, I strongly recommend reading *Irreversible Damage* by Abigail Shrier.

It is worth noting that not every parent that has a gender-confused child is a "Munchausen by Proxy" parent. It is possible for a child to become gender confused in a lot of the ways. This can include the Internet, schools, and forms of media. Some parents find out about their kids' gender preferences, and they genuinely don't know what to do. But they try to have their child's best interest at heart. Because of this, there are two ways to distinguish a "Munchausen by Proxy" parent from a regular parent.

The first way to tell is to consider the age at which the child experiences gender confusion. If a child experiences gender confusion in their teens, then it is probably not the parents' fault. As mentioned above many forms of media can influence a child. For example, TikTok is a popular social media platform for kids. Some activists on TikTok can confuse kids. So, it is possible that the confusion can come from sources other than the parent.

However, if the child experiences gender dysphoria before the age of five, that is a good indication of a "Munchausen by Proxy" parent. This is a good indication because the parent is the primary influence on the child. So, if the child is having ideas of gender confusion, it's probably the fault of a parent. In the case of Jazz, some parents have said their kid was transgender before the child could even talk.

The other way of checking is to see whether or not the parents advertise their kids on social media. The "Munchausen by Proxy" parents are seeking validation through virtue signaling. So, they will likely have their child's story plastered all over social media or other forms of media. This is similar to the poser parent, but these parents will focus on their child's LGBTQ traits. If the child didn't have these traits, the parents probably wouldn't be showing them off.

And to anyone who says, "There's no way I could convince my child they are a member of the opposite sex."

To them I ask, "Have you ever met a small child?" Children are easy to influence. Every year, children are convinced that a Coca-Cola-drinking fat man, with flying reindeer, gives them free presents on Christmas. It's disgusting that these parents take advantage of their child's trusting nature for their own benefit. It is even more disgusting that the benefit is usually nothing more than social media attention and validation. All for the small cost of their child's mind, body, and soul.

## Conclusion

When I first heard the Aaron Clarey quote at the beginning of the chapter, I could not believe that he had hit the nail on the head so perfectly. According to Pew Research, 23% of children will grow up in a single parent household in the United States. "In comparison, 3% of children in China, 4% of children in Nigeria and 5% of children in India live in single-parent households. In neighboring Canada, the share is 15%[67]. That's right folks, Canada tops the U.S. in something besides hockey and maple syrup.

And even if parents are willing to marry, how long does that last? According to Forbes, 17% of couples with two children experience divorce, 13% of married couples with three kids divorce.[68] As I mentioned back in Chapter 2, the only reason that people should marry is to provide a stable environment for their kids, but modern American parents can't even get that right.

The "your parents love themselves more than they love you" quote doesn't necessarily mean that your parents *don't* love you. But ask yourself this. Did your parents love their career more than they loved you? Did your parents care about booze more than you? Did your parents love you enough to put aside their petty bullshit and fulfill their duty to you as parents? Did your parents love you more than their hot secretary or sexy personal trainer? Did your parents care more about having nice things than spending time with you? Did your parents even care enough about you to get married in the first place?

If you answered all these questions correctly, congratulations! You had good parents. And this section of the book probably doesn't apply to you. Treat your parents well and take care of them in their old age. At the very least, spring them from the nursing home on occasion to get them away from Nurse Ratchet. For everyone else, you do not owe your parents a damn thing. There is no sacrifice in making a baby. Two people had sex and that led to you. The real sacrifice comes from parents who work hard and provide for you. And if your parents failed in that regard, you owe them nothing.

Clarey often sarcastically thanks American parents for doing such a terrible job. Because if they did a good job, he'd be out of business as an "Asshole Consultant." An "Asshole Consultant" is what it sounds like. If you have problems, personal or business related, you pay him, and he answers your question. No kid gloves, no BS. If you need to hire him, contact him at assholeconsulting.com. Clarey has heard and shared many stories about crappy parents. One of the stories that he talks about most involved a single mom who threatened to disown her son if he joined the military. this was not out of some antiwar sentiment but because she would lose Section 8 housing if he left home. She was willing to restrict her son's future for her current benefit. But that sort of selfishness is something that doesn't surprise me anymore.

If you don't want kids, use whatever birth control methods you can find. Forms of temporary, non-hormonal birth control for men are now in the developmental stages. If you do want kids, make sure that you're a good parent to them. Especially if you didn't have good parents growing up. Regardless of whether you want kids, do what you can to break the cycle of crappy American parenthood.

# Reason 4: Authoritarianism Has Arrived

"Screw Your Freedom."

—Arnold Schwarzenegger

Of all the things wrong in American society today, I think everyone can agree that authoritarianism has arrived. Conservatives will look at the left and see threats to First and Second Amendment rights. Liberals compared Donald Trump to Hitler for four years. The only disagreement is about who is the more oppressive authoritarian.

I always believed that Americans would not stand for petty authoritarianism and certainly not any sort of burgeoning totalitarianism. I had hoped that the spirit of our Founding Fathers would ring true, and we would unite against those who would oppress us. I did not count on the amount of division that the United States would endure. This partisanship has solidified into a seemingly permanent "us vs. them" mentality. And of course, this division is used by politicians and media figures to convince people to submit to authoritarianism.

The COVID-19 pandemic demonstrated Americans' willingness to submit. What started with two weeks to slow the spread became a two-year fiasco, even though a vaccine had been created after roughly eight months.

People who spoke out against this were shamed and deplatformed. There could never be any dissent against the so-called experts. The best example of this was in March of 2021. The governor of Florida, Ron DeSantis, held a panel discussion talking about the COVID-19 policy and potential policies the state could implement. On the panel, DeSantis was joined by Dr. Scott Atlas of Stanford University, Sunetra Gupta of Oxford University, Dr. Jay Bhattacharya of Stanford University, and Martin Kulldorff of Harvard University.[70] The conversation shifted toward whether children should wear masks. Atlas, Bhattacharya, and Kulldorf said in so many words that children should not have to wear masks. Because of that YouTube removed the video, citing medical misinformation. "The Centers for Disease Control and Prevention recommends that children 2 years and older wear masks. The agency also recommends that children wear masks in schools, childcare settings and any environment when they are around people who don't live in their home."[71]

The right of a platform to censor has become a topic of debate over the last couple of years. Ultimately, it comes down to making the distinction between platforms and publishers. Publishers have full control over what they choose to publish. Because they have such control, publishers are liable for everything they choose to publish. If the *New York Times* were to intentionally publish something false about a public figure, the paper could be sued for defamation.

Platforms are different than publishers because they are designed to be open forums where everyone can speak. Platforms have some ability to regulate content. These regulations are typically aimed at things like pornography, controlling spam, and summons to engage in hostile activities (call to violence). Because a platform does not have final say over what is posted, it is not liable for any harm or misinformation. For example, it is not Facebook's fault if a bunch of idiots start rumors that Hillary Clinton worships Satan and drinks the blood of children.

The censorship of DeSantis is something else entirely. This was a sitting governor discussing health-related policies. And he was actively censored because the panel members disagreed with CDC recommendations. If these companies wish to control content so extensively, they should be treated as publishers, not as platforms.

Going back to COVID-19. One of the memes that floated around the Internet was to trust "the science." But it seems few people understand the purpose of scientific discussions. Science is not obedience to a given hypothesis: That's called religion. Science is the gathering of data and information to prove or disprove various theories or hypotheses. There is no such thing as science through consensus. A thousand years ago everyone thought that the earth was flat and at the center of the universe.

Today, we know that children were not at risk of dying from COVID-19. How do I know this? The final CDC death count for 2020 was a total of 350,831.[133] What was the number of children under the age of fifteen that had COVID-19 listed as the underlying or contributing cause of death in 2020? According to the CDC: 134,[71] which means that children accounted for 0.0381%, which means approximately 99.96% of deaths were by people other than children.

Anytime someone mentioned a possible treatment for COVID-19, the media would come up with some ridiculous story to try and discredit the person. One of the first potential drugs for treatment was hydroxychloroquine. It was believed that with a combination of drugs, hydroxychloroquine could reduce the symptoms of COVID-19. Then president Donald Trump had talked about it as an effective treatment. In all fairness to the media, hydroxychloroquine was not proven effective, and more time was needed to assess its effectiveness. If the media wanted to effectively caution the public against calling hydroxychloroquine a cure for COVID-19, media outlets simply would have said, "The drug's effectiveness is being examined; it's too early for optimism. But we will keep you informed as this develops." Instead, media outlets went in a much different direction. NBC told a story about how a woman and her husband were poisoned by hydroxychloroquine, but they weren't taking pills. The woman and her husband drank fish tank cleaner.

Here is an excerpt from the NBC article: "An Arizona man has died after ingesting chloroquine phosphate—believing it would protect him from becoming infected with the coronavirus. The man's wife also ingested the substance and is under critical care. The toxic ingredient they consumed was not the medication form of chloroquine, used to treat malaria in humans. Instead, it was an ingredient listed on a parasite treatment for fish. The man's wife told NBC News she'd watched televised briefings during which President Trump talked about the potential benefits of chloroquine. Even though no drugs are approved to prevent or treat COVID-19, the disease caused by the coronavirus, some early research suggests it may be useful as a therapy."[72]

When Joe Rogan talked about taking ivermectin for COVID-19, the media responded in a similar fashion. CNN said that Joe Rogan was taking medicine found commonly in horse dewormer. While it is true that ivermectin is effective in treating parasites, the story was framed as if Rogan was going to Pet Smart and gobbling up medication for horses. Yet Rogan was taking medicine prescribed by a doctor.[69] It did lead to some funny memes though. My favorite was one of a CNN anchor saying, "Joe Rogan spotted drinking a liquid commonly mixed with engine coolant." And in the next picture, Joe Rogan is drinking water.

People were quick to go along with government rules and regulations. Even if the regulations did not make any sense, you had to wear a mask when you were at a restaurant, but you could remove the mask as you ate your food. Elderly people in nursing homes died alone in some corner room. Many of these people, despite being the most at risk, would have been willing to risk COVID-19 if it meant they could see their loved ones. Public parks and playgrounds were shut down. In April of 2020, Sara Brady was arrested for taking her children to a public park[133]. It was even known at the time that COVID-19 did not survive or spread well in a warm and humid environment. So, an outdoor playground posed little to no risk of infection.

And it went beyond people following rules and regulations. Some people derived personal value from following the rules. Masks became more of a political statement than a statement for public health. People who protested masks and lockdowns were shamed by media outlets. The best example of this is when CNN's Don Lemon went on a rant about people who were angry at the lockdowns. Dismissing the people protesting lockdowns as people who just want a haircut. '"You're slapping the face of the people—the health care workers who put their lives on the line every day because you want a haircut, you want to go play golf- of course you're concerned about your business. Tell the president that!" Lemon shouted. "And you're out there with guns? With weapons strapped to your chest, saying you're fighting against the people trying to tell you to stay at home, trying to save your lives? You're upset with those people? In the meantime, there are people who are keeping your cities going, keeping your loved ones alive, and you want to get a haircut? Who the hell do you think you are?!? What is wrong with people?!? I don't understand what is wrong with people!"'[73]

The media's coverage of COVID-19 was irresponsible and borderline fear-mongering. People online began to call the coverage of COVID-19 "COVID panic porn." The result is that you had a terrified population. There were people who would wear their masks when they were by themselves in their cars. There was even an article about a guy who would not take off his mask at all, even during sex.[74]

All this shows a feedback loop between media figures and government officials. The media creates fear, and the government will abuse their power to combat the problem. And this goes above mask mandates and social distancing. In November of 2021, the Biden administration tried to impose a nationwide vaccine mandate for all businesses that have over a hundred employees. As well as a mandate for all medical facilities that accept Medicare, all employees had to be vaccinated. I remember one guy I worked with in Montana nearly quit because he was worried about getting the vaccine. And the lab was already short staffed.

The Biden administration released the announcement on November 4, 2021. "First, the Department of Labor's Occupational Safety and Health Administration (OSHA) is announcing the details of a requirement for employers with 100 or more employees to ensure each of their workers is fully vaccinated or tests for COVID-19 on at least a weekly basis. The OSHA rule will also require that these employers provide paid time for employees to get vaccinated, and ensure all unvaccinated workers wear a face mask in the workplace. OSHA has a strong 50-year record of requiring employers to take common sense actions to prevent workers from getting sick or injured on the job. This rule will cover 84 million employees.

Second, the Centers for Medicare & Medicaid Services (CMS) at the Department of Health and Human Services is announcing the details of its requirement that health care workers at facilities participating in Medicare and Medicaid are fully vaccinated. The rule applies to more than 17 million workers at approximately 76,000 health care facilities, including hospitals and long-term care facilities."[75]

This was taken to the Supreme Court, which struck down the first mandate from OSHA. The court approved the second part for medical workers being vaccinated.[76] The second mandate passing is not a concern. Government entities have the right to dictate terms to people who get government funding. You may not agree with the policy, but the government is within their rights on this mandate. It's just another example of developing a rash after getting into bed with the government.

The first mandate is where the real problem lies. The first mandate would have given outsized power to the Executive Branch of the government, transforming OSHA from a government entity that ensures workers are given proper safety equipment and instructions to an entity that can control nearly every aspect of a private venture.

The biggest difference between conservative and liberal judges is that conservatives try to remain bound to the constitution. All three of the liberal judges, Stephen Breyer, Sonia Sotomayor, and Elena Kagan approved both measures of the mandate. And keep that in mind for other cases I discuss throughout the chapter, that we may be only three judges away from absolute authoritarianism.

But the authoritarianism problem goes even further than this. It goes beyond government imposing tyranny on its subjects. Citizens now seek to impose tyranny on other citizens and are willing to use any means necessary to do it.

Masterpiece Cakeshop is a good example of this. You have likely heard of this case. In 2012, Jack Phillips, owner of Masterpiece Cakeshop, did not want to bake a cake for a gay wedding. The owner cited religious reasons for not wanting to. The couple sued Masterpiece Cakeshop for violating the Colorado Anti-Discrimination Act. Part of the Colorado Anti-Discrimination Act states that there shall not be any discrimination for "place of public accommodation." That refers to any place of business engaged in any sales to the public and any place offering services, facilities, privileges, advantages, or accommodations to the public.[15]

This led to the Masterpiece Cakeshop, Ltd. v. Colorado Civil Rights Commission case at the Supreme Court. The court ultimately ruled in 2018 in favor of Masterpiece Cakeshop. Since then, Masterpiece Cakeshop has faced another legal challenge. In 2021, A customer wanted to order a cake to celebrate a "gender transition." Masterpiece Cakeshop refused. It was likely that Masterpiece Cakeshop was targeted by this activist and knew that Phillips would refuse. Masterpiece Cakeshop was sued again under the Colorado Anti-Discrimination Act. Jack Phillips was ordered to pay $5,000 in fines. He will likely appeal the decision, and the case will probably end up in the Supreme Court.

Ultimately, this conversation is centered on the fine line between freedom and discrimination. Do Americans have the freedom to discriminate? Yes and no.

Section 1 of the Fourteenth Amendment to the Constitution says, "All persons born or naturalized in the United States, and subject to the jurisdiction thereof, are citizens of the United States and of the State wherein they reside. No State shall make or enforce any law which shall abridge the privileges or immunities of citizens of the United States; nor shall any State deprive any person of life, liberty, or property, without due process of law; nor deny to any person within its jurisdiction the equal protection of the laws."[16]

The Fourteenth Amendment guarantees that all citizens of the United States are granted equal protection under the law. That means this amendment regards every citizen as equal under the law and cannot choose favorites. In truth, the United States should not have had to adopt civil rights legislation: the Fourteenth Amendment should have protected American citizens from racial discrimination and, for example, Jim Crow laws. State governments had no right to discriminate against its citizens.

A state cannot mandate legislation and then discriminate against its citizens with the execution of that legislation. Say that a state mandates that everyone over the age of eighteen gets a state-sponsored driver's license. The state cannot then mandate that black people be denied service at DMVs or be charged more money for the service. This is because the state created a mandate and has a monopoly on the service. You can't walk into a Walmart and pick up a driver's license. In this scenario, the state showed an unlawful bias. Any form of discrimination that comes from public office to private citizens is unlawful and unconstitutional. The government cannot show favoritism to one group over the other and still consider the groups equal.

While public discrimination is unconstitutional, the same cannot be said for private discrimination. Private discrimination is the discrimination between two parties that have nothing to do with the public or state. The Masterpiece Cakeshop case above is an example of this.

The state of Colorado has no right to dictate to Jack Phillips how he should conduct his business. What happens between Mr. Phillips and his customers should stay between the two parties.

When a business provides a good or service, it is not binding until both sides agree to the terms. If someone offers to cut your grass for $30, you have the right to accept or deny the service. But just because the service provider makes an offer to the public does not mean you are entitled to it. The service provider still reserves the right to refuse service for any reasons. The service provider pays for this by losing the $30 in revenue.

Jack Phillips made an offer to sell baked goods to the Colorado people. It is up to him to decide whose business he wants. If he does not want to sell cakes for gay weddings or gender transition parties, that is his right, so long as he is willing to accept the loss in revenue. That loss in revenue should be the only thing that Jack Phillips should worry about losing. I would argue that in trying to dictate who Jack Phillips serves violates the equal protection clause in the Fourteenth Amendment. By saying that these customers are entitled to the services of Jack Phillips, you are saying that the two parties are not equal. They are not equal because you are taking preference over the customers' rights rather than the rights of Jack Phillips.

Just as Coloradoans are not entitled to Jack Phillips' services, Jack Phillips is not entitled to the business of Coloradoans. The Colorado legislature cannot pass a bill that mandates people spend at least $30 a week at Masterpiece Cakeshop. To do so would be unfair to the Coloradoans.

A lot of people who support the customers in the case argue, "Well why don't you just bake the cake? It's not that big a deal." But the customers who are suing Jack Phillips are broaching an issue larger than cakes. Those customers believe that they are entitled to Jack Phillips's time and services. Unless a contract has been agreed to between two parties, no one is entitled to another person's time. But these people are willing to use the force of the government and any other institution to push their beliefs on others.

It's not enough that homosexuals can get married today. If these authoritarians get their way, you will celebrate it. You will bake the cake. One way or another.

I always find it amazing when TV shows predict the future. Just as The Simpsons predicted the presidency of Donald Trump, South Park predicted the cultural intolerance that we see today. In the South Park episode, "The Death Camp of Tolerance," fourth-grade teacher Mr. Garrison is acting very gay in the classroom. He is doing it so that he can get fired and sue the school for discrimination. Just to give an example of one of the things he does, he gets a fellow gay man as his assistant teacher and proceeds to shove a gerbil up his assistance's ass. When the boys complain about this to their principal and their parents, they are deemed intolerant and sent to a tolerance camp.

The tolerance camp is a parody of Schindler's List. When the boys are at tolerance camp, the scene is in black and white, and a bunch of Germans are forcing the boys to make arts and crafts that demonstrate their tolerance. As the head of the camp said in a German accent, "Here you will work, every hour of every day. Until you submit to being tolerant of everybody. Here intolerance... will not be tolerated."

In January of 2023, NHL star Ivan Provorov of the Philadelphia Flyers caused controversy when he did not wear a pride shirt that celebrated the LGBTQ community. Provorov is a Christian and felt that wearing apparel that supported this community went against his beliefs. When asked about it he said, "I respect everybody's choices. My choice is to stay true to myself and my religion."

This caused outrage among activists and journalists. There were calls for the Flyers to be fined $1 million for the outrage. One sportscaster even suggested that he should go back to Russia.

To be fair, this exists on the American right as well. When San Francisco quarterback Colin Kaepernick kneeled during the national anthem a few years ago, there were people who wanted to see him fired. Although it's also fair to say that the national anthem is (or at least used to be) more unifying than an LGBTQ celebration.

Tolerance does not mean that you celebrate something. If you're looking to be celebrated, the word you are looking for is *accepted* or *revered*. Tolerance is simply existing with something that you may not like or agree with. Ivan Provorov said that he respected everybody's choices. He simply did not wish to celebrate.

But even if governmental or cultural forces do not compel you, there is still one more way to get society to bake the cake. Through the children. The best example of this is the Hitler Youth. In the 1930s, The Nazis used Hitler youth to indoctrinate children to follow the Third Reich. It was effective because the Nazis were able to get the children away from their parents and any other influence. By 1939, over 90% of German children were a part of the Hitler Youth organization.[17] One man recalled, "I belonged to Adolf Hitler, body and soul."

The United States does not have anything as evil as the Hitler Youth, but there is the American education system. It turns out that the education system isn't just good at wasting students' time. It's also good for indoctrinating children into certain ideologies. There are teachers who are perfectly fine introducing LGBTQ+ propaganda in schools. That is essentially what the Libs of TikTok Twitter account does. The account will take stories and videos of left-wing activists and share it among people on the right. The Libs of TikTok are able to do this because these teachers and activists do not hide the ball. Many of these teachers will go online and brag about their exploits.

There was one YouTube short[77] where one teacher believed she was spreading transgender propaganda through transgender dinosaur stickers to children. What's a transgender dinosaur sticker? A cartoon dinosaur sticker with light blue and pink colors. She was proud of what she was doing, saying that the students loved her stickers. Those kids probably didn't even know what those stickers represented. I wouldn't have realized what those stickers represented if she hadn't said anything.

Extremely graphic and sexually themed books have targeted children in school libraries. Some people defend giving these graphic books to children; it is depressing. In 2023, an eleven-year-old Maine student read from a book that was on display in his school's library. Below is most of the passage that he read:

"My back over my hips. I asked if he should take his clothes off. He was saying yes before I finished my sentence. He's pulling off my T-Shirt, laughing when I can't undo his shirt buttons. He's undoing my belt. I'm reaching into his bedside drawer for a condom. We're kissing again. We're rolling over. Obviously, you can see where this is going. I don't know if it's because we are feeling especially emotional or just tired or these past couple of weeks have been too much. But this reminds me so much of the first time we had sex. We were both fucking terrified and the whole thing was kind of terrible because we didn't know what we were doing. But it was good too".[18,19]

The excerpt is from the book *Nick and Charlie,* which is about early teen boys who sexually experiment with each other.

You would think that a teacher (or someone) would have seen the boy with the book and said that it was not age appropriate for him. You'd be wrong. The librarian allegedly saw him with the book and asked him if he wanted more and if he wanted a graphic novel version.

And this isn't something that politicians are shying away from. The Democratic Party has made it abundantly clear that they are in favor of this sort of indoctrination for children. As the former Democrat Virginia governor Terry McAuliffe said in a debate, "I'm not going to let parents come into schools and actually take books out and make their own decisions," adding, "I don't think parents should be telling schools what they should teach."[78] People like McAuliffe have stated that they do not believe that parents should have any rights about their children's education. But this goes beyond education. This is about teaching a morality to children that the parents may oppose. They see this as an opportunity to influence children in a cultural direction that they believe will benefit them politically. And when parents push back against this, these politicians will fight hard to ensure that the indoctrination keeps going.

When the Florida State Legislature put forward the Parental Rights in Education Bill, teachers, activists, and politicians nearly lost their collective minds. They referred to the bill as the "don't say gay bill." Here are three headlines from various publications:

In *Time,* "What to Know About Florida's New 'Don't Say Gay' Rule That Bans Discussion of Gender for All Students"[79].

By NPR: "Florida's governor signs controversial law opponents dubbed 'Don't Say Gay'"[80]

By Meredith Johnson from Georgetown Law: "The Dangerous Consequences of Florida's 'Don't Say Gay' Bill on LGBTQ+ Youth in Florida"[81]. The headline assumes the bill was designed to ostracize homosexuals in Florida public schools, but that wasn't what the bill was about.

A summary of the bill states the following:[20,21] "The bill (Chapter 2022-22, L.O.F.) reinforces a parent's fundamental right to make decisions regarding the care and upbringing of his or her child in the public-school setting. The bill requires each district school board to adopt procedures for notifying a student's parent if there is a change in services or monitoring related to the student's mental, emotional, or physical health or well-being. All procedures adopted under the bill must require school district personnel to encourage a student to discuss issues related to his or her well-being with his or her parent. The bill prohibits a school district from maintaining procedures that require school district personnel to withhold from a parent, or encourage a student to withhold, information related to a student's mental, emotional, or physical health or well-being. School district procedures may authorize school district personnel to withhold information only for a reasonable belief that disclosure would subject the student to abuse, abandonment, or neglect."

There is also a section in the bill that seeks to prevent the introduction of inappropriate material to students. "Classroom instruction by school personnel or third parties on sexual orientation or gender identity may not occur in kindergarten through grade 3 or in a manner that is not age appropriate or developmentally appropriate for students in accordance with state standards." That's right, activists were upset because teachers could not introduce sexual orientation or gender identity concepts to children under the age of nine. And they did not want parents to know what was going on with their children in the classroom. They are in favor of having pornographic material in libraries and encouraging kids to read it. Maybe I am showing my age here, but when I was a kid, these people would have been labeled as creeps and perverts.

Some schools allow for teachers and school administrators to socially transition children (meaning treat them as the opposite sex) at school and not inform their parents about what's going on. Schools can call children by different names, give them different clothes to wear, address the children by different pronouns, all without informing the parents. And this is not a red versus blue state issue. According to the *New York Post*, "More than 3.2 million US public school students are covered by guidance that blocks parents from knowing whether their child identifies as a different gender in the classroom... At least 168 districts governing 5,904 schools nationwide have rules on the books that prevent faculty and staff from disclosing to parents a student's gender status without that student's permission, according to a list compiled by the conservative group Parents Defending Education and shared with the Post. The 3,268,752 students affected by such policies go to class in all kinds of districts — large and small, affluent and poor, urban and rural, red and blue — stretching from North Carolina to Alaska."[134] This bill requires teachers and school administrators to inform the parents about these issues relating to their children. Is that so bad?

And it goes beyond what schools are teaching kids. Other activists are trying to push a social agenda message on small children. Disney is now pushing this activism on kids. Disney executive Latoya Raveneau stated that she had a "not at all secret gay agenda." Saying, "In my little pocket of Proud Family Disney TVA, the showrunners were super welcoming . . . to my not-at-all-secret gay agenda... Maybe it was that way in the past, but I guess something must have happened . . . and then like all that momentum that I felt, that sense of 'I don't have to be afraid to have these two characters kiss in the background.' I was just, wherever I could, adding queerness. . .. No one would stop me, and no one was trying to stop me."[82]

A few years ago, an episode of the kids' show *Blue's Clues* celebrated pride month.[83] It featured a drag queen singing about families that had two moms, or two dads, two nonbinary parents, and two transgender parents.

The San Francisco Gay Men's Chorus even sings a song about how activists will convert your children. Below are most of the lyrics to the song.[22]

"You think we're sinful/ You fight against our rights/ You say we all lead lives you can't respect/ But you're just frightened/ You think that we'll corrupt your kids/ If our agenda goes unchecked/ Funny, just this once, you're correct/ We'll convert your children/ Happens bit by bit/ Quietly and subtlely/ And you will barely notice it/ You can keep them from disco/ Warn about San

Francisco/ Make 'em wear pleated pants/ We don't care.../We'll convert your children.../We'll make them tolerant and fair/Just like you worried\They'll change their group of friends\ You won't approve of where they go at night (to protests)/Oh, and you'll be disgusted(so gross)/When they start finding things online/That you've kept far from their sight(like information...)\Guess what?\You'll still be alright!\We'll convert your children\Reaching one and all\There's really no escaping it\'cause even grandma likes Rupaul\And the world's getting kinder\Gen Z's gayer than Grindr\Learn to love\Learn to vogue\Face your fate!\We'll convert your children\Someone's gotta teach them not to hate\We're coming for them\We're coming for your children\We're coming for them\We're coming for them\We're coming for your children\For your children."

It's not shocking that these people are going after kids. A child's mind is like wet clay. The younger the child, the wetter the clay. In *Animal Farm* by George Orwell, the animals rebel against their farmer. The animals begin to run the farm themselves as a socialist society. The pigs become the ruling class of the farm. Two pigs, Napoleon and Snowball, differ in their approach to the animal farm,. While Snowball spends his time planning and organizing ways to improve the farm, Napoleon spends most of his time raising a litter of puppies. Napoleon is able to brainwash the puppies into his way of thinking. When they become grown dogs, Napoleon uses the dogs to chase Snowball off the farm and seize control.

Like Napoleon, these activists are going after kids. They're looking to gain control over the future. And these people aren't very keen on the idea of American freedom and liberty. Like I said, you will celebrate, and you will like it. How long before the United States starts trying to push hate speech laws? You say it's unconstitutional? Out of everything that I have written in this chapter, what makes you think that these activists care about the Constitution, or the rights of others?

There is authoritarianism coming from the right as well. This can be seen with the Conservative-dominated Supreme Court overturning Roe v. Wade. Let me preface this by saying that there is no "right to an abortion." You can flip, turn, and look at the Constitution with a Cracker Jack decoder ring. You will not find an amendment in the Constitution that says that a woman has a right to terminate her pregnancy or kill her unborn baby, regardless of which side of the argument you fall on. In fact, I would argue that Roe v. Wade was a terrible ruling that violated the Tenth Amendment to the Constitution. "The powers not delegated to the United States by the Constitution, nor prohibited by it to the States, are reserved to the States respectively, or to the people."[84]

This means the issue of abortion in the United States is a *state* issue. Different states can impose different restrictions or lack of restrictions based on the will of the people living in that state. Places like Florida can put forward bills that ban abortions after six weeks. Places like California or New York can have abortion laws that are available going into the third trimester. And states can't influence other states' laws. Florida can't influence California's laws and vice versa.

Challenging Roe v. Wade was something that prolife conservatives had desired for decades. But what happened once conservatives finally achieved this victory? U.S. Senator Lindsey Graham (R-South Carolina) put forward a federal abortion bill that would federally restrict abortion in the U.S. "The legislation would set a federal minimum protection for unborn children that is in line with European limits and ban abortion after 15 weeks gestation when unborn children can feel pain."[85] Regardless of whether or not you agree with these standards, this shows willingness of the right to engage in authoritarianism as well.

# Reason 5: Young People Are Lied to About the Opposite Sex

> The truth always comes out in the end, no matter how hard anyone tries to hide it. Lies are just a temporary delay to the inevitable.
>
> — Unknown

The term "red pill" has become popular in the past few years. Some people try to associate it with politics or culture, but the red pill is simply about trying to see past the lies of society. The term "red pill" refers to a scene in *The Matrix*. In the now famous scene, Keanu Reeves's character Neo is told that the world he perceives is not the real world. Neo is given the choice to take a blue pill or a red pill. If he takes the blue pill, he will continue to live in the fake world that surrounds him. If he takes the red pill, he will awaken from this false reality and know the truth of the world.

That's probably the most famous scene in the movie. It represents a man who is actively choosing to leave a false reality and live in the real world. But there are subtle details in the movie that are equally important. When Neo is offered the red pill, he is told by Morpheus, "Remember. All I'm offering is the truth, nothing more." But Neo's curiosity about the matrix and the real world compelled him to take the red pill and awaken from his false reality.

Neo was shown the truth about a post-apocalyptic world that was run by machines. He was horrified. Morpheus then told him, "I didn't say it would be easy, Neo. I just said it would be the truth." It is hard to live in the real world. It can be a cold, mean, unforgiving place that will consistently try to knock you down.

Today men use the "red pill" to share experiences and information on what is referred to as the "manosphere." In the manosphere, there are different voices with different messages for men. These voices can range from pick-up artists, to men going their own way (MGTOW). People discuss male and female psychology. A lot of the conversations are about men and women's interactions in the sexual marketplace.

The sexual marketplace is not a brothel or a sex market. It's just a concept to show the interactions between men and women. These interactions range from hooking up, dating, or even marriage.

All of the lies in this chapter have to do with the sexual marketplace. These lies are told to both men and women. Some of these lies may simply be bad advice. Others are given by people who have absolutely no idea what they're talking about. Many of these lies are based on complete equality of the sexes, meaning that men and women are the same. Contrary to many people's beliefs, men and women are different. And what men desire in women is different than what women desire in men. The first lie is one that is told to many women.

Lie: A woman's career is her best-selling point in the sexual marketplace.

This first lie is more of a miscalculation than an outright lie. But there is some influence of third wave feminism and its attempts to redefine and change gender roles. Young women are told to go to college, find a career, and not settle down when they are young. The last one is the most damaging of the three. This is something that women have taken to heart. The median age for first weddings among women was 28.6 in 2021. The median age for a woman's first wedding in1998 was 25. [23]

The idea that "a woman's career/education is her best selling point in the sexual marketplace" is rooted in the lie that "men and women are the same." And the idea is not an illogical one. The thought process goes along the lines of, "I want a man who is educated, successful, driven, ambitious, etc. For me to be able to find a man, I need to have these qualities." Having career success and/or being educated is important to women. The ability to gather and manage resources is one of the ways that female hypergamy has operated throughout human history. But this is not as important to men when they are seeking a woman.

So, what is the main thing that men seek in women? Men seek youth and beauty. That is a woman's number one asset in the sexual marketplace. Christopher Rudder is the Cofounder of Ok Cupid and author of the book *Dataclysm*. In *Dataclysm*[24] Rudder used data from Ok Cupid to chart the age that men find women most attractive. In one chart, Rudder compares a man's age to the age of the women who look best to him. The men's ages range from twenty to fifty years old. All of the men found women to be most attractive within an age range from twenty to twenty-four years old. The data showed that twenty-two-year-old men found twenty-one-year-old women most attractive. Thirty-seven-year-old men found twenty-two-year-old women most attractive. And forty-five-year-old men found twenty-four-year-old women most attractive.

This differs from women's age preference regarding the age of men who look best to her. Most of the data points are within a five-year window. For example, twenty-year-old women found twenty-three-year-old men most attractive. Thirty-year-old women found thirty-year-old men most attractive. And forty-year-old women found thirty-eight-year-old men most attractive. This suggests that differences exist in male and female sexual market value (SMV).

Male and female potential sexual market value (SMV) comes from Rollo Tommasi in *The Rational Male*.[26] Tommasi used graphs to show the potential SMV of men and women from ages fifteen to seventy-five. You can also see the graph at https://therationalmale.com/2013/06/20/smv-ratios-attachment/). If you look at the graph, you will see that a woman reaches her potential sexual market peak in her early twenties. She will peak at around age twenty-three and remain at that same potential SMV until her mid-twenties. At around age twenty-seven, her potential SMV will begin to decline. And it will continue to decline throughout her thirties.

Theman's potential SMV is different. A man's potential SMV remains pretty low throughout his twenties. This is mostly due to the man being inexperienced and having to gain wisdom in the world. As he becomes more established and makes a name for himself, his potential SMV rises. Men and women's potential SMV meets at the same level around age thirty. The man's potential SMV continues to rise and peaks in his mid-thirties.

But men and women are on the same level when they are thirty. Why is that not a good time for a woman to try to find a man? The problem with this line of thinking is that you are not considering the female competition. A high-value, thirty-year-old man isn't just going to get attention from thirty-year-old women. He is going to get attention from women in their early and mid-twenties. So, you have women in their mid-thirties competing against women in their early-to mid-twenties. And because men tend to favor younger women, it is not a favorable matchup for women in their 30s.

This results in women being extremely confused in their thirties wondering why they are getting less attention than when they were younger. I saw a video clip that portrayed this confusion perfectly; it was from *The Steve Harvey Show*. The video showed a woman in her mid-thirties. She had a successful career; she was educated, and very ambitious. But she didn't have a husband, and she wanted to have kids. She was trying to figure out what she was doing wrong. She had a successful career. It was quite sad to see this woman in tears from her confusion and frustration. I have a great deal of sympathy for this woman because she had the idea that men and women wanted the same thing, and she has to suffer the results of her miscalculation.

This is not universal and does not apply to every woman. These concepts do not suggest that once a woman hits thirty, it's an automatic game over. The purpose of the *Dataclysm* and potential SMV charts is to demonstrate that a woman who is thirty-two will likely receive less attention from men than that same woman would have when she is twenty-five. The twenty-five-year-old woman will be in a better position to (for a lack of better word) market herself according to the consumer's desire (i.e., men).

Say you are looking for a restaurant. And the most important thing to you is the price of the food. Then you see a commercial for a local restaurant. The commercial says that the restaurant has the highest quality food in town, a warm and friendly atmosphere, and a friendly staff with smiles on their faces. But nowhere in the commercial does it mention anything about price. The most important aspect that you are looking for was not mentioned. These aspects maybe important to some people, but it's not the main selling point that you are looking for. So are you going to go to that restaurant? Probably not.

And that's the same problem that the woman from the *Steve Harvey Show* faced. She was trying to sell the wrong thing. And because she was in her mid-to-late thirties, her chances of getting a husband and kids were not very good. And that's true for multiple reasons. Her potential dating pool was a lot smaller because a lot of men her age were already married. And she had to compete against younger women. And even if she was able to find a husband, there is no guarantee that she could have kids by the time she found him.

Now, this is not to say that a woman cannot have an education, a business, or a career. But if a woman wants a family, she needs to focus on that in her early twenties. Like men, a twenty-year-old woman could have fifty years to fulfill her career ambitions. A woman can start a new job when she is thirty. She can go to school when she is forty. I had female classmates over the age of fifty at LSU. In that time, she can fall, make mistakes, and start over. When it comes to having a career, time is on the side of women. But time is not a luxury for a woman who is wanting to start a family.

A woman has roughly ten to fifteen years to start a family. And the best years are front loaded in that time frame, not only due to men preferring younger women, but due to the decline in female fertility over time. According to Forbes Health, "Age is indeed a factor affecting female fertility rates. Not only can age impact a woman's ability to conceive—becoming pregnant without medical intervention is unlikely by the age of forty-five; having a baby later in life can also increase the risks of complications in pregnancy . . . A woman's fertility generally begins to decline at around age thirty-two, and then drops off more dramatically after age thirty-seven. For couples in their twenties and early thirties with no known preexisting conditions, around one in four women will get pregnant in a single menstrual cycle. By age forty, that number drops to one out of every ten women."[86]

A woman who starts looking earlier in life will have more time to find someone to marry. After all, a twenty-three-year-old woman who loses out on a two-year relationship doesn't suffer the same cost as a thirty-year-old woman. She will have a higher quantity and quality of options to choose from in her early twenties than she will in her early thirties. If youth and beauty is something that men want, women should use their youth and beauty as leverage in the sexual marketplace to get the best deal possible.

Lie: Women Want Nice Guys

I would define a nice guy as "a man whose main point of value is his high-level of agreeableness." For years men have been told that women love the nice guys. This is a lie that rings true for a lot of millennials. Due to the rise of social media and the manosphere, I don't think younger men are falling for this lie as much as previous generations. The "be nice" lie was usually told to us by teachers, maternal figures, and media figures.

One of the best examples of this was an episode of *Johnny Bravo*. The episode was called "The Sensitive Male!" and it aired in 1997. For those that never watched the show, Johnny Bravo is a silly, muscular man who is always hitting on women and looking for dates. He typically approaches women by showing off his muscles and talking about himself, but he often gets rejected. In this episode, Johnny approaches a woman with his usual smug behavior and gets rejected. But shortly afterward, a short, fat, bald, sensitive man gives the woman flowers and asks her in a very passive manner to go out with him. The woman immediately falls for the guy. When Johnny asks the guy how he got that girl to like him, he decides to coach Johnny on how to get women. Throughout the episode, the man gives Johnny advice such as, "Be sensitive, don't be too masculine, use your manners, etc." The twist at the end of the episode was that the guy didn't believe any of what he was saying; he just pretended to be sincere. And when the women found this out, they were not happy with the liar. But it still gave the message that women would fall for a guy that was in touch with his feminine side.

Boys were told, "It's OK to be sensitive. Share your feelings. Be gentle. Girls appreciate nice guys." And young men fell for this lie because it makes logical sense. After all, would you want to consistently be around someone who is mean to you? No, you'd want someone who is loyal, genuinely cares about you, and appreciates you. However, there is evidence to suggest that women are not really into the nice, sensitive types.

A study in the UK[87], showed a correlation between dark triad personality traits and female attractiveness. The three Dark Triad personality traits are narcissism, psychopathy, and Machiavellianism. In the study they define each dark triad personality trait as the following: "Narcissism is defined by a sense of entitlement, dominance and a grandiose self-view...Machiavellianism is associated with social manipulation and opportunism, both beneficial to the pursuit of short-term mating... Psychopathy consists of callousness, a lack of empathy, and antisocial, erratic behavior"[87]. In the study, each subject with high amounts of Dark Triad personality traits were given higher rates of attractiveness by the women. In the conclusion of the study, the research team says, "In conclusion, the results of our study demonstrate that the Dark Triad male personality is attractive to women and this effect is not mediated by these men's greater perceived Extraversion or Neuroticism. Further work in the sexual marketplace could usefully pursue interactions (statistical and social) between sellers (Dark Triad men) and buyers (women)."[87]

This lie is the male equivalent of the saying, "A-woman's-career-is-her-best-selling-point-in-the-sexual-marketplacelie." And this lie has the same result. The people who are lied to will feel a sense of confusion and frustration. And who could blame them for feeling this way? They did what they were supposed to do. So why are they not getting the results that they crave? These feelings cause young men to start to realize that they were lied to.

You could say that when you see through this lie, you are at least somewhat red-pilled. A lot of young men today may have been red-pilled by guys like Andrew Tate. For those who do not know who Andrew Tate is, he is a social media influencer who gives dating and life advice for men. I personally don't follow Andrew Tate, so I couldn't tell you much more than that. What red-pilled me was an article called, "Six Harsh Truths That Will Make You a Better Person." I remember reading this and wishing that I'd come across it when I was sixteen.

The article is meant for young men who may not have a lot of experience in the world or men who are confused about their place in the world. The main point of the article is that when it comes to men, the world only cares about the value you bring to it. And this is true throughout all of society. This is true for future employers, friends, and even women.

Employers don't care about your personal history. They want to know whether or not you can get the job done. When looking for friends, you may not think to yourself: "How can I benefit from being friends with this person?" But you will ask yourself whether this is the kind of person that you enjoy being around. Or if this person will be there to help you when you need it. One of my favorite lines from the article is, "'So, what you're saying is that I should pick up a book on how to get girls?' Only if step one in the book is, 'Start making yourself into the type of person girls want to be around.'" The article asks readers if they are funny, interesting, or charming. Other people's reactions to you are a pretty good measure of these things. If you constantly make other people laugh, chances are you are funny on some level. The main point of the article is that being nice is pretty much the bare minimum. I strongly recommend every young man read the article.

This goes hand-in-hand with what a lot of men in the manosphere talk about. They talk about going to the gym, getting in shape, and having skills that will benefit men outside the dating scene. That goes well with the idea that women seek men with value.

A quote that has been shared in the manosphere is one by Sheryl Sandberg. "When looking for a life partner, my advice to women is date all of them; the bad boys, the cool boys, the commitment phobic boys, the crazy boys. But do not marry them. The things that make bad boys sexy do not make them good husbands. When it comes time to settle down, find someone who wants an equal partner."

What this quote suggests for women is to completely ignore the nice guys when they are in their early twenties. Those are also women's sexual peak market years. When she is in her later twenties, she should find a nice guy and marry him. This strategy is commonly used in the United States today. As I mentioned earlier, the average age of women marrying for the first time has increased over the last twenty years. So, a woman who dates the bad boys in her early twenties, but then looks to settle down with a nice guy at twenty-eight follows the Sandberg approach.

I think the results of the Sandberg approach are best summed up by Chris Rock: "Women don't like nice guys. Say they do. Don't! They have got to have an asshole first. Every woman goes through an asshole phase. They gotta go out with Ike then Mike. That's right! You know what's bad? If you a nice guy, like me, you always get woman after they've they're out with an asshole. So now you gotta be their boyfriend and their psychiatrist, to help them get over this psycho. That's right! For every twenty minutes of pussy, three hours of therapy!"

Lie: It is empowering for women to treat sex like men do.

Here is a big lie that has been pushed by modern feminism. Over the last fifty years, feminists have tried to blur the lines between men and women. They have done this by encouraging men to be more feminine and women to be more masculine. And in a way they have succeeded. As I noted back in Chapter 1, "Women can't even define the term 'woman.'"

One of the ways that feminists have made women more masculine is by encouraging women to be more promiscuous. One hundred years ago, this would not have been possible. Female biology would have hindered women's promiscuous behavior. Birth control was limited at that time, and with society being more conservative, women tended to be more cautious and reserved. These things are why the single motherhood rates were low. According to the Washington Post, "the current figures contrast sharply with 1960, when only 9% of children lived in single-parent households. In that year, 93% of white children and 75% of black children lived in two-parent homes."[88]

But, with advancements in birth control, pregnancy is not as big a concern for a woman who takes her reproductive control seriously. However, even with the risk of pregnancy minimized, it is not wise for women to be oversexualized. As is how later in the section, it is devaluing to women. The idea that it is empowering for a woman to sleep with lots of men is fallacious in three ways.

First: Having the power to do something doesn't always mean that you should do it. You can drink a gallon of vodka every day. But you will likely face health complications in the long run due to liver disease. And there will be men who won't want a long-term relationship with a woman with a promiscuous past.

Second: It's not empowering to simply give the opposite party you are negotiating with everything that they want. There was a Key and Peele comedy sketch a few years ago. Keegan Michael Key was dressed up as a fictitious pop star. He was supposed to look like a woman, but Key has a masculine appearance, so the audience must suspend disbelief that anyone would think he was a woman (this was prior to Dylan Mulvaney). There are a lot of sexual themes in the popstar's songs.

Key's character takes a couple of questions from some young women in the audience. The first girl said that she followed the popstar's lyrics but ended up losing her virginity to a guy she didn't even know. Key's character then goes on to say that it's time for women to take back their power and feel sexy and empowered. The girl then says that she is pregnant. Key's character replies with, "Miracles! Next Question."

The next question had a similar outcome. A woman followed the popstar's lyrics and got an STD (sexually transmitted disease) from it. Key's character ducks the question and goes to "her" dressing room. While in front of a mirror, Key removes his wig. Shockingly, it was a man the whole time. While looking into the mirror, Key says in a low and creepy voice, "That's right girls. Being overly sexual and being strong are the same thing. It's the same thing." He then proceeds to laugh maniacally.

The third fallacious reason is that it assumes that men and women operate with the same set of goals and parameters in the sexual marketplace. But that's not the case. Men and women are different and want different things. To demonstrate the differences between men and women in the sexual marketplace, I'm going to apply some basic economic theory to sexual marketplace properties.

I am going to show a couple of graphs. Each graph will be different in the appearance of the supply and demand curves. There will also be differences in supply and demand representations for each graph. But I want you to pay attention to the points where supply meets demand or the 'equilibrium point.'

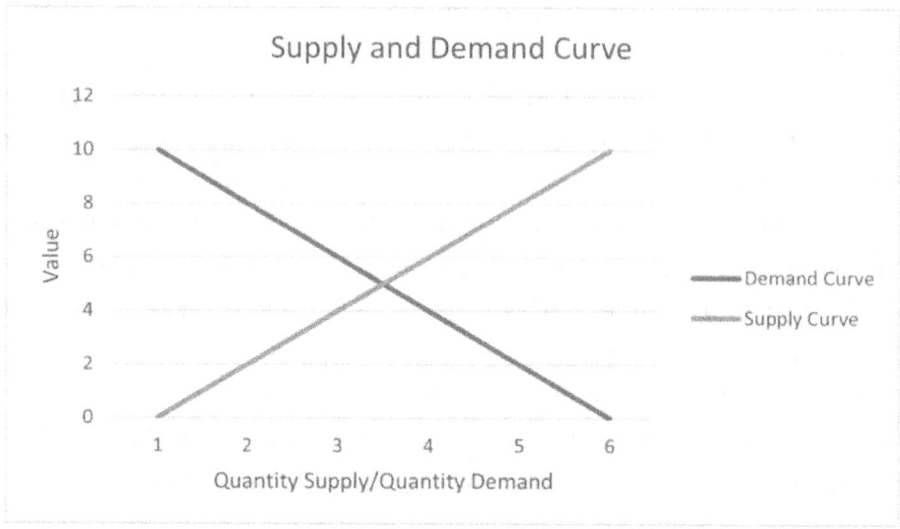

The above graph is a basic linear supply and demand curve. The demand curve is the downward sloped line, and the supply curve is the upward sloped line. The Supply curve and the Demand curve meet at a "Value" (measured on the Y axis) of approximately 5. The Quantity Supplied and Quantity Demand (measured on the X axis) is approximately 3.5 units. Again, the point where the Supply Curve and Demand Curve intersect is called the Equilibrium Point. It shows the ideal conditions for the market under the current circumstances. For this example, a Supplier is providing 3.5 units of a good or service to a consumer in exchange for 5 units of value per item. I also want to demonstrate what an increase in supply and increase in demand will look like for these curves.

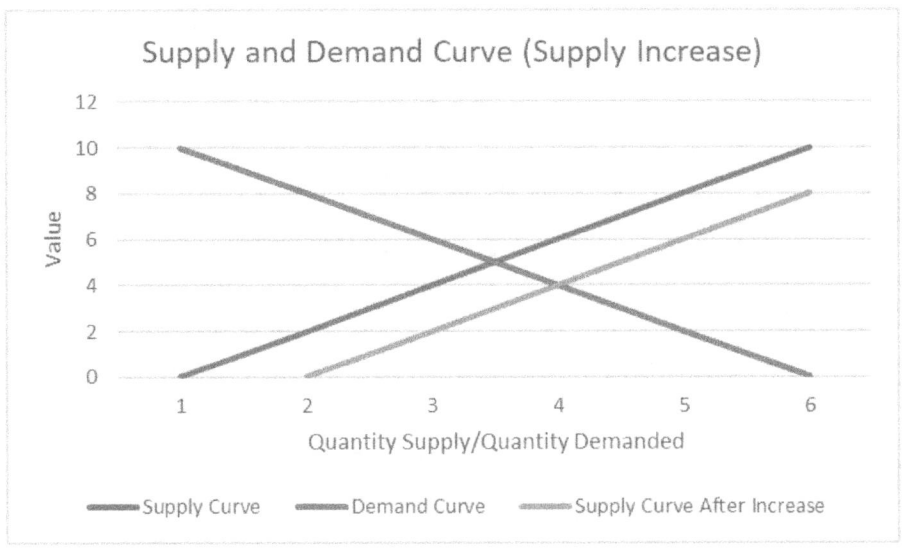

The above graph represents an increase in supply. In this example, the initial supply curve (the line that has quantity supply of 1 when value equals zero) increases. When the supply increases, the new supply is represented by the parallel line to the right of the original supply curve. You will note that the equilibrium value has decreased. Before the increase, the equilibrium value was approximately 5 (initial supply meets demand curve). After the supply increases, the new equilibrium value is 4 (new supply curve meets demand curve). This demonstrates that an increase in supply, while keeping all else constant, will decrease the value of something in the marketplace.

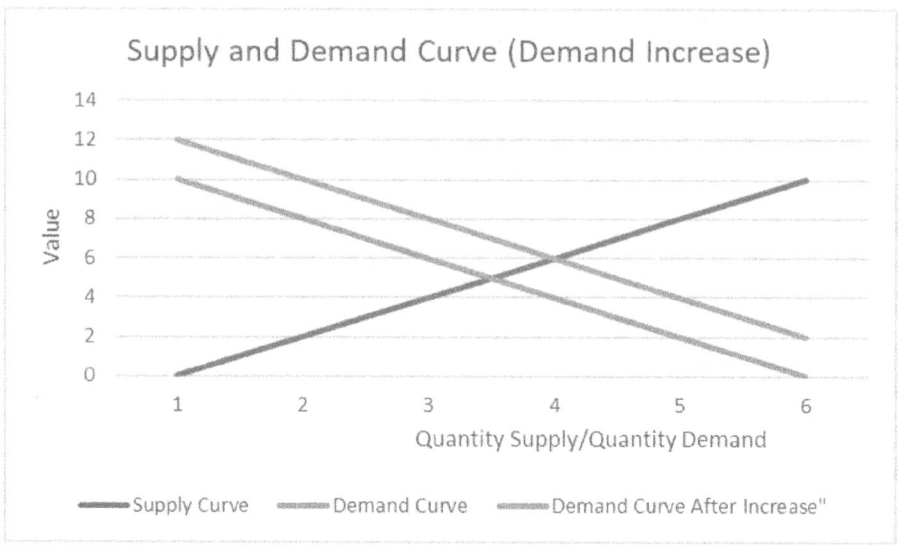

I also wanted to demonstrate what an increase in demand looks like. The original demand curve is the lower downward sloped line. For this curve the higher downward sloped line demonstrates an increase in market demand. The new demand curve is represented by an upward shift in the original demand curve. After this shift, the equilibrium value increased. The original equilibrium value (lower downward sloped line meets upward sloped line) was 5. After the demand increase, the new equilibrium value (higher downward sloped line meets upward sloped line) is 6. This demonstrates that an increase in demand, while keeping all else constant, will increase the value of something in the marketplace.

In typical supply and demand curves, value is usually represented by price. However, I wanted to be consistent with my labels to avoid confusion. In the next two graphs, "Value" will represent the sexual market value. "Value" does not represent any sort of personal worth or value to society. The term "sexual market value" refers to the amount of sexual interest that one draws from the opposite sex. Sexual interest is the service that is being supplied and demanded. Since women are the gatekeepers of sex, women will represent the supply curve. Naturally, men having the stronger sex drive, represent the demand curve. I also want to note that these graphs are merely used as a visual aid. They do not represent any real data set.

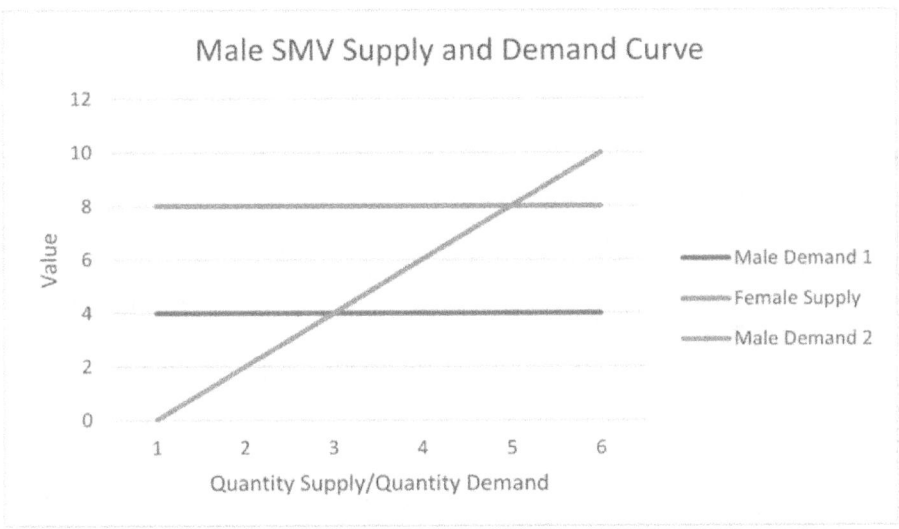

In the graph above, you will notice some changes. The two demand curves are flat. The reason the demand curves are flat is to demonstrate that value is fixed in the short term. This means that it takes time for a man's value to change. It is not like a grocery store where the owner could change the prices every other minute if they desired. For a man to change his value, he needs time in order to shift the demand curve upward.

For now, don't worry about the top horizontal demand curve; it will make sense later. One important thing to note: In the male graph, the demand curves represent the quantity demand for sex of one male; the Female Supply represents the total supply from the entire female population.

Here is an example to help you make sense of the graph. You have a man, who on a scale of one to ten, is a 4 in sexual market value. First, he represents the bottom horizontal line. At his current value, three women are interested in him (bottom horizontal line meets upward sloped supply curve). However, the man does not like his results. He starts to exercise; he gets a better job, and improves his social skills. This increases his value as represented by an upward shift in the demand curve. His demand curve is now represented by the top horizontal line. Keeping everything else constant, due to his increase in value, he now has access to a higher number of women. The point where the top demand curve meets the supply curve is now at around 5. This means that in the same passage of time, more women are now interested in him.

Now let's see what the Female SMV Supply and Demand Curve looks like.

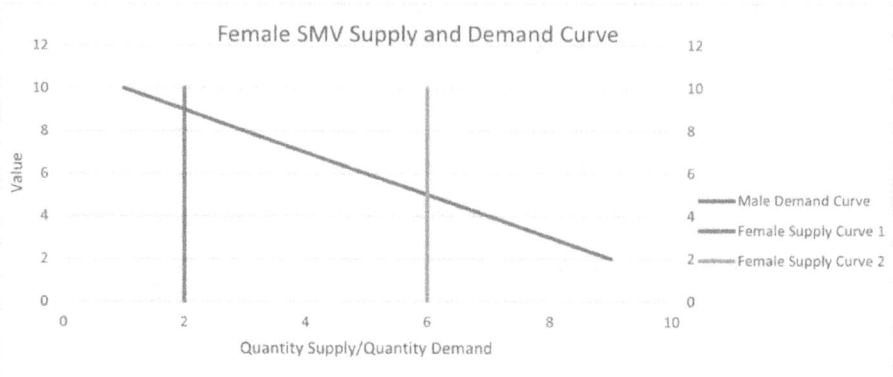

In this graph, you will note that the demand curve is similar to the first graph. However, the supply curves are vertical instead of curves with a positive slope. The supply curves are vertical because this assumes that the supply of sex one woman can provide is fixed in the short run. This means that it takes time for a woman to find a man. In this graph, the demand curve represents the entire male population's demand for one female. The female supply curves represent the amount supplied by one female. Unlike the male SMV graph, a woman can use two factors to affect her SMV: the amount of the supply and the demand curve.

Even though a woman represents the supply curve, she can increase her SMV by affecting the demand curve. This is like the way men increase their demand curves. Do things that will attract the opposite sex. Women can do several things to increase the demand curve and their SMV as a result. The two things a woman can do to increase or maintain a high demand curve is to avoid single motherhood and obesity.

Single motherhood can not only lead to permanent poverty but also dramatically reduce a woman's dating opportunities. In a study done by Date Psychology[89], the men surveyed responded negatively to single mom dating profiles. Seventy-eight percent of men had a negative response if the women had kids. Forty-five percent said that a woman with kids was an absolute deal breaker for them, meaning the men would reject the profile no matter how attractive the woman was. If a woman is going to be sexually active, it is advised that she approaches sex and the risks that come with it accordingly.

Men also tend to prefer women with lower body fat percentages. A study performed by Macquarie University,[90] showed that men tended to prefer women with lower percentages of body fat. '"According to previous health studies, the healthy body fat range for young Caucasian women is 21 to 33%. "Our participants optimized a healthy-looking body composition for women at around 19% fat, and a most attractive-looking body type of just 16% fat. However, there was no difference in the amount of muscle preferred for healthy-looking and attractive bodies. This suggests that while previous studies have found that smaller female body size generally corresponds to a greater perceived attractiveness, this observation is actually due to people's preference for lower fat mass, rather than lower muscle mass or smaller body size in general,' explained research-group leader Dr Ian Stephen, also from the Department of Psychology."[90]

Going back to the female supply and demand curves, the graph compares a woman with all other variables kept the same. The only difference is the supply (number of sexual partners). The left vertical line represents the initial supply. At this equilibrium point (where the left vertical line meets the downward sloping line), the woman's sexual market value is approximately 9. The right vertical line represents what the woman's sexual market value would be with an increase in supply (number of sexual partners). As you can see, the supply curve shifts to the right of the original curve. At this new equilibrium point, where the new supply curve crosses the demand curve, the value has decreased to around 5 as the supply has increased. This demonstrates the effects of a decrease in value as supply increases while keeping all else constant.

So, what does this demonstrate? For starters it demonstrates that female hypergamy is real. Hypergamy is a woman's desire to be with the best option she thinks she can get. And there is nothing wrong with hypergamy. Hypergamy makes logical sense because women face greater risks from sex. Contrary to the opinion of trans activists, men cannot get pregnant. Either that or we have all hit "manopause." Hypergamy is demonstrated in the male's sexual marketplace graph. The man who increased his sexual market value was able to get more opportunities. The man will keep the interest of the women who were originally interested in him, but as he gained value, he drew the interest of more women.

It also demonstrates that men do not prefer women with a higher number of sexual partners when it comes to long-term relationships. The female sexual marketplace graph shows that when all else is kept constant, men place higher value on women with fewer sexual partners. The reason that men prefer women with fewer sexual partners is due to a man wanting to ensure paternity of their children. Before paternity testing was available, men would judge a woman's behavior to try to determine her propensity for cheating. This was to lessen the chance of paternity fraud.

Paternity fraud is when a man is tricked into raising a child that he believes is his biological offspring. But due to a woman's infidelity, the child is not biologically his. Paternity fraud is something that women will never understand. When a woman gives birth, she knows that the child is hers. But many men have been victims of paternity fraud. According to the National Library of Medicine, different studies show a rate of paternity fraud between 0.8% and 30%.[27] And even with paternity testing widely available, the problem persists today.

You may say that someone should not be judged for their past behavior, but we do this in many ways in our society. When you apply for a loan, what do they check? They check your credit history, your work history, your assets, and your liabilities. Would you give a loan to someone who defaulted on their last three loans?

And it doesn't have to be an act of promiscuity. Even the appearance of a promiscuous past can drive men away. For this reason, I would also advise women to stay away from the pornographic industry. Only Fans or any other amateur pornographic platform is something that may seem lucrative for a lot of women. But because it can give the appearance of a promiscuous past, men will be less willing to commit long term to those women.

The point of this section was to show that there are differences between men and women in the sexual marketplace. The assumption that it's empowering for women to be as sexually promiscuous as men is fallacious and damaging to women. This "empowering behavior" will only result in women wasting their best years. Which brings me to the final lie.

Lie: You are guaranteed a lifelong partner.

I once heard someone say, "Capitalism is like consensual sex. I got something you want, and you got something I want. So, let's get together and make a deal. "It's a funny line. But it does show that the sexual marketplace, like all marketplaces, requires two consenting parties to operate, and both parties need to have something that the other party wants.

In this chapter, I have mentioned the lies that men and women hear regarding what the other group wants. For men, it's not enough to be nice. The "seven harsh truths" article says that being nice is the bare minimum. It's like going to a restaurant with the slogan, "The food will not make you sick." Men have to provide value in some way or another. Are you attractive, funny, interesting, educated, or charismatic?

But that is true even if men desire a lifelong partner. There has been a growing movement in men called "men going their own way" or MGTOW. If you ask a hundred people about that group, you will probably get a hundred different opinions. Some people will say that it's a bunch of losers that spend all day playing video games and are angry that women don't want to be with them. Others will say that they are a bunch of men who have faced divorce and family court and don't want to be with anyone as a result. And another group will say that they are men who are not interested in getting married or having kids. Regardless of what people say, men in MGTOW, for one reason or another, have decided not to seek a lifelong partner.

Not having a life partner is also affecting women. Morgan Stanley projects that "single women are expected to grow +1.2% annually from 2018-2030 compared with+0.8% for the overall U.S. population" And "45% of prime working age women(ages 25-44) will be single by 2030—the largest share in history—up from 41% in2018."[28] Now this does not mean that all women in this group will remain single forever. But if the graphs by Rollo Tomassi and Christopher Rudder are to be believed, the women in their late thirties and forties will have more trouble than women in their twenties. And will likely remain single.

I know that it may have come as a surprise, but men have standards and preferences as well. As I said earlier in the chapter, men prefer women intheir twenties. Men don't like women who constantly berate them and talk down to them. And men prefer women who are physically fit.

Some people will probably say, "I don't like the fact that men have a higher demand for young, in-shape women, who are pleasant to be around." OK, well, I don't like that there is a market demand for heroin. The truth is that you don't have to like something for it to be a reality. And like I said back in Chapter 1, reality has a way of winning every time.

And that's the truth about any marketplace. The consumers (demanders) cannot force the firms (suppliers) to meet their exact demands. Just as the firms cannot force consumers to purchase their products, there is usually a series of compromises that ideally lead to supply meeting demand and reaching a market equilibrium.

But lies have created illusions about what the other party wants. And that leads to people pursuing things that the other party is not interested in. And what's the result? It has led to men checking out of the dating market and going their own way. And it has led to women being like the woman from the *Steve Harvey Show* that I mentioned earlier: women who wanted to have a family but were lied to about the amount of time required to achieve this and about the desires of men. These lies will ruin the lives of many men and women.

Conclusion

So, what does all this have to do with the downfall of the United States? Intersexual dynamics are important for maintaining and growing a population. Since 2007, birth rates in the United States have consistently declined. 2020 saw the lowest birth rate ever recorded in the United States, an average of 1.641 births per 1000 women. The lowest it had ever been prior to this was in 1976 with 1.738 births per 1000 women. And the COVID-19 pandemic did not seem to have a big impact. In 2019, there were 1.706 births per 1000 women. And the rates remained low post pandemic. In 2021, there were 1.664 births per 1000 women.

Can I attribute low birth rates to all the lies in the chapter? No. Since the birth control has become more available in the United States, birth rates have been lower.[91] But from 1976 to 2007, there was a birth rate range of1.738 births per 1000 women to 2.120 births per 1000 women. To say that birthrates have consistently dropped throughout the 2010s suggests that other forces are at work.

A possible explanation for low birth rates in the 1970s was rough economic times. The years 1970, 1974, and 1975 saw periods of economic recession,[91] as well as high inflation rates. But the 2010s saw a decade of economic growth with low inflation rates. So, you can't blame the economy. Regardless, entitlement programs such as Medicare and Social Security rely heavily on a large, young population base. Due to low birth rates among the millennials, as well as government reluctance to reform these programs, these programs will face financial troubles in the future. If you are a millennial or GenZ, I suggest planning retirement around your personal retirement goals.

# Reason 6: Societal Standards Have Fallen

"We cannot live better without seeking to become better."

–Socrates

I often find myself longing for the days of my adolescence. I'm not saying that I would want to be a child again. Rather, I'd want to live in the world of the late 1990s and early 2000s. I'm not saying the world was perfect. The United States was engaged in the war on terror; technology wasn't as advanced; Hurricane Katrina devastated New Orleans, and there was always some form of partisan divide in the country.

But the incentives in our society seem to have shifted. Twenty-five years ago, would you have imagined young women being actively encouraged to engage in pornography or content creation for OnlyFans (as it is also called). I remember a lot of women wanting to be singers but not overt sexual objects for men's pleasure.

I will also say that the standard of beauty was a lot higher when I was a kid. Circa 2005 Jessica Simpson was probably thought to be the most beautiful woman in the country. She was also an actress and a singer. If she was the standard of beauty at the time, that was a hard standard to meet. Today, you have a morbidly obese fat activist and singer Lizzo, saying she's the beauty standard. That's not an exaggeration; in a video, she also said, "I am fucking gorgeous. I am the beauty standard."[92]

I wish she were lying, but unfortunately, the standards of beauty have considerably declined. According to the CDC, "From 1999–2000 through 2017–March 2020, U.S. obesity prevalence increased from 30.5% to 41.9%. During the same time, the prevalence of severe obesity increased from 4.7% to 9.2%."[140] Obesity has become even more prevalent in the United States. People don't care about how they present themselves to the world. And it doesn't even have to involve a person's BMI.

***

In the summer of 2022, I visited family in New Jersey. My cousin, her family, and I went out to eat lunch. As we were riding in the car, I saw something strange. I noticed a lot of people were wearing pajama bottoms while they were walking around the streets. I asked my cousin (one of the sweetest ladies I've ever met) why so many people were wearing pajama bottoms. She told me that pajama bottoms were part of the style. I just sat there in stunned silence.

I've seen some people wear pajamas in public before. If I saw someone wearing pajamas at a pharmacy, I'd probably assume that they are sick and getting medicine before going home. I have also seen people wear pajamas at the doctor's office. Of course, these were sick patients and were more concerned with getting healthy than looking good.

But I've also seen people wearing pajama bottoms in other locations. I have seen people wear them at the grocery store while shopping for food. I have also seen people wear them at the airport. I remember talking to my coworker Dana about this. She called the pajama bottoms "the given-up-on-life pants." After all, it wouldn't take too much effort to throw on something classier than pajamas. And it is not just about wearing something tacky. There have been tacky fashion trends in the U.S. before. Trends such as parachute pants or disco medallions. But people were at least putting effort into the way they presented themselves to society.

This was the first time that I heard of pajamas being "a style." I may not be a fashion expert, but I'll tell you this. Wearing pajama bottoms in public isn't part of a style. It's being lazy.

Compare this to the way things used to be. There is a YouTube channel called "NASS." The channel remasters old footage of places like San Francisco and Los Angeles around the 1940s. The footage is even in color. It's quite astonishing. You see people well dressed, clean, hygienic, and walking with purpose. And this is not an issue of economics. Even when people were standing in bread lines during the Great Depression, people were well dressed. Even when people didn't have enough money for food, they still put their best foot forward. The issue is not one of economic class; it's an issue of a lack of class.

Are these declines in fashion standards going to destroy America? Probably not. It's just something that makes old man Mebruer upset. But there is a decline that I have not mentioned yet. And that's the decline in American morality.

A recent example of this is Satan Con 2023 in Boston. The irony is that that many of these people don't worship Satan. To do so would require belief in a God or Satan. It's just a bunch of anti-religious amoral fools. If you look at the "Temple of Satan" website, one of its pamphlets reads, "The Satanic Temple practices non-theistic Satanism; we believe that religion can, and should, be divorced from superstition. As such, we do not believe in either God or the Devil as supernatural forces"[141]. They are also cowardly. At this convention, people tried to be edgy and tore out the pages of the Bible. What's a Christian going to do? Pray angrily at you? If you want to be ballsy, try tearing out the pages of a Quran. I don't think Muslims will take that crap.

America's moral decline is due to moral relativism. Moral relativism is the idea that there are no moral absolutes in the world, and that leads to self-serving chaos. The state of parenthood in the United States is one of moral relativism. After all, being a parent is hard. And we wouldn't want to judge people who miserably failed as parents . . . right?

Yeah . . . I'm sure the complaint, "It's hard to be a parent" is real comforting to the kids that have to live with the results of their parent's failures and derelictions of their parental duties.

I once heard a "complex" moral scenario about a man leaving a country to live in another country. He had large amounts of credit card debt before he left and decided not to pay the amount he owed. The credit card country would be unable to find him, so there would be no consequences for his actions. He felt that because the credit card company was so large, it could take the loss, and it was a victimless crime.

The scenario is not complex. This man was wrong. He is a liar and a thief. Not only did he break his agreement with the credit card company, an agreement that he made in good faith, but he also stole from the credit card company. The outcome would have been exactly the same if he stole the balance amount from the credit card company and used it to purchase goods. He's what economists call a "free rider." More on that in Chapter 8. In short, the term "free rider" is from an economic concept called "the prisoners' dilemma." The prisoners' dilemma goes like this. Two people, person A and person B, are arrested for a suspected crime. The two are put in separate interrogation rooms. Each is given two choices, to snitch on the other person or not to snitch. Both are incentivized to snitch because they are promised reduced sentences if they snitch on the other person. However, there will be a higher collective utility if both do not snitch.

The potential outcomes are the following. If person A and B do not snitch, then both will be convicted of a lesser crime and spend two years in jail. If person A snitches and person B does not snitch, then person A will go free and person B spends ten years in jail. If person B snitches and person A does not snitch, then person B will go free and person A will spend ten years in jail. If both parties snitch on each other, both will spend seven years in jail.

A free rider is someone who accepts the benefits of something without helping, adding any value, or having any intention of adding value to the system. This is usually done at the expense of others. The man who cheated the credit card company may think his actions are not free of consequences, but that's not the case. If enough people break their agreements, then the credit card company will have to make up for its lost revenues by raising interest rates or making new fees. They will pass the burden on to others.

But the real issue has nothing to do with the one man's thievery and a credit card company. It's the fact that moral relativism has convinced people that immoral actions are okay as long as it is against acceptable victims.

Moral relativism in America is hitting new lows. One of the most disturbing pieces of data is how young people (ages 18-24) reacted to the October 7,

2023 Hamas terror attack on Israel in 2023. In this attack, Hamas targeted civilian populations, inflicting egregious war crimes on civilian men, women, and children. Not only did Hamas kill 1200 people, but they also raped and murdered many women.

Yael Richert, a superintendent with the Israel Police, said the following, "There were girls with broken pelvis due to repetitive rapes, their legs were split wide apart in a split... We heard girls that were pulled out from the shelters. Girls that shouted. They raped girls. Burnt them just after that. All the bodies outside were burnt."[142]

United States Secretary of State, also commented on the attack. Saying, "It's impossible for me to look at the photos of families killed – such as the mother, father, and three small children murdered as they sheltered in their home in Kibbutz Nir Oz – and not think of my own children... This was just one of Hamas's countless acts of terror – in a litany of brutality and inhumanity that, yes, brings to mind the worst of ISIS. Babies slaughtered. Bodies desecrated. Young people burned alive. Women raped. Parents executed in front of their children, children in front of their parents."[143]

These acts were not the acts of collateral damage that is often seen in war. It was personal and intentional. I hoped that the American people would look at this depravity and condemn it entirely. Young Americans did not see it the same way. A Harvard Harris poll[144] asked two questions.

1. "Do you think the Hamas killing of 1200 Israeli civilians and the kidnapping of another 250 civilians can be justified by the grievances of Palestinians or is it not justified?"

2. "Do you think that the attacks on Jews were genocidal in nature or not genocidal?"

Sixty percent of people aged 18-24 and 4% of people aged 25-34 said that the acts of terror were justified. The fact that these people excuse the raping and murder of women and children is disgusting.

And you can't say that the people were ignorant of the situation. When asked, "Do you think that the attacks on Jews were genocidal in nature or not genocidal?" Sixty-six percent of people aged 18–24 agreed that the acts were genocidal in nature, which means that there is a group of people in this country that will not only excuse the raping of women and the murder of children; they will also justify acts of genocide.

It's disheartening to see America's future lacking in sense and morality. And its moments like these that are bound to make some people wonder, "If this is our future, is America even worth saving?"

# Reason 7: Men Are Checking Out

"A lot of men are trash."

—Tomi Lahren

One of the best stories demonstrating a young man's journey into manhood is *Sleeping Beauty*. In the final act, Prince Phillip is locked in the dark castle of Maleficent. The evil Maleficent taunts Phillip by showing him a ruined kingdom that was his to inherit and a beautiful young princess Aurora, who is held captive to Maleficent's cruelty. Maleficent had cast a spell on the kingdom which made everyone in the kingdom sleep. She plans to keep Phillip for a hundred years so that she can keep the kingdom in constant sleep. Only Phillip can break the spell, so Maleficent will only let Phillip go free once she feels she has had her revenge against the kingdom.

Prince Phillip is trapped in the dark prison and is unable to act against his captor, but he is rescued by the three fairy godmothers who represent the human conscience. They free him from his shackles and his prison cell. They arm him with a shield of virtue and a sword of truth. As Phillip escapes the castle, he is confronted with many obstacles, but with the assistance of the fairy godmothers (his conscience), he escapes Maleficent's prison. He then rides out to save the princess and his kingdom.

The evil witch Maleficent continues to throw obstacles Phillip's way. Phillip must overcome her magic and the henchmen throughout his journey. But he is determined. And with truth and virtue he continues to overcome the obstacles until, finally, only Maleficent stands in Phillip's way.

Maleficent menacingly blocks the path. And she calls on the vile forces of hell to oppose Phillip. She takes the form of a dragon, a symbol of chaos. As she transforms, Phillip is visibly terrified when he sees the dragon, and yet he does not turn and run. Armed with truth and virtue, he boldly charges against chaos.

Phillip is immediately knocked off his horse by Maleficent. He must endure this final battle alone. Phillip struggles to avoid the fire and jaws of chaos until with his sword of truth, he is finally able to pierce the heart of the chaotic beast and win the day.

He climbs the tower and finds Princess Aurora. And with true love's kiss, the kingdom is saved. And what was Phillip's reward for all the hardships he endured in his battle? He gains the admiration of his kingdom, his father's respect, and the love of a beautiful woman.

It's a great story that highlights a young man's journey. A young man is trapped in his youthful and idealistic ways. But as he ventures forth into the world, he faces struggles and hardship. With a good conscience, he battles the chaos of the world. And in doing so, he is changed as the harshness of the world diminishes his idealistic nature. But what he loses in innocence, he gains in wisdom. And he is then able to take his place in society so that everyone can benefit from his experience.

Now there is something to note that many people don't understand. Phillip had to fight against many obstacles in his way. His value came from what he was able to provide. In this case, he saved the kingdom from Maleficent, creating order from chaos.

But what was Princess Aurora's role? All she did was sleep while under the influence of a curse. And yet, she was the prize that Phillip was willing to slay a dragon for. But why? Where does this value come from? The truth is that women have an inherent value that men do not have.

We men are tools of society. And like any tool, we must bring value and purpose, or else we are cast aside. As it says in the Bible (Matthew Chapter 7 verse 19), "Every tree that bringeth not forth good fruit is hewn down and cast into the fire. Wherefore by their fruits ye shall know them."

It doesn't sound good or fair to be the disposable sex. But don't be angry about it. That's like being mad at gravity. It's just the way the world has operated for all of human existence. It is why men were chosen to hunt woolly mammoths with rocks and pointy sticks. It's one reason why men have usually been the frontline soldiers throughout history. And it is why Phillip had to slay the dragon to rescue the princess.

Where do you think you would be if you were on the Titanic? The women and kids are considered the valuable ones. They are the ones that get on the lifeboats. If you were a man, you were probably going down with the ship. And if you managed to find a piece of buoyant debris, you had to give it to a woman. And the two of you couldn't share the makeshift raft. You must stay in the icy water and freeze to death so that Rose can have her elbow room.

So, why do we do it? Because appreciation comes with the sacrifice society demands of us. As men labor and sacrifice, they are rewarded with loving families and societal appreciation—two things that appeal to most men. But as American society evolved, it has demonstrated a gradual decline in the need for men.

Feminism has demonstrated this over the last fifty years. After all, "a woman needs a man like a fish needs a bicycle." And give credit where it's due. Feminism and social media have done something that has been nearly impossible to do throughout history: Make men more reluctant to pursue women. According to a 2022 Pew Research study,[119] over 60% of young men (age 18 to 29) are single. The same study showed that roughly 50% of single men are looking for some kind of relationship (either a casual or a committed relationship). If that distribution holds true for single men aged 18 to 29, then nearly one in three young men is single and not seeking any type of relationship.

I am sure that several factors play into this. I would argue that feminism, social media, promiscuity, increases in obesity, mental illness, and single motherhood throughout the twenty-first century has made many women unappealing. Even the most basic of expectations will significantly affect a man's potential dating pool. A young man seeking a woman who is in shape and does not suffer from a noticeable mental illness will have limited options.

Nearly 40% of women aged 20 to 39 years old are classified as obese. This includes women that are severely obese (11.9% of women). [120]

Mental illness is also limiting options. The National Institute of Mental Health defines any mental illness (AMI) as "a mental, behavioral, or emotional disorder. AMI can vary in impact, ranging from no impairment to mild, moderate, and even severe impairment." Severe mental illness is defined as "a mental, behavioral, or emotional disorder resulting in serious functional impairment, which substantially interferes with or limits one or more major life activities."[121] Over 40% of women aged 18 to 29 suffer from some form of mental illness.[122] Fortunately, the percentage of women suffering from *severe* mental illness is lower. Between 12.8 and 16.9% of women aged 18 to 29 suffer from severe mental illness.

If you take obesity and mental illness rates into consideration, more than half of a man's dating pool can be excluded. And that's not considering other things such as values, religion, personality, hobbies, etc. This could be one reason why "men going their own way" or MGTOW could be popular. Even though newspapers like the *Guardian* try to label MGTOW as something "toxic,"[124] it's just a bunch of men who have lost interest in dating and would rather spend time with friends and enjoy their hobbies.

I said back in Chapter 2 that marriage and the family unit are two critical institutions of American society. I still stand by that statement and fully recognize the importance of the two. The reason that I understand men's hesitancy toward marriage is because of the laws and procedures that entail marriage in America today. I have seen and heard many horror stories of men getting absolutely wrecked in divorce and family court.

I have known many good, honorable men who worked hard to care and provide for their wives and children, only to be tossed aside when their wives decided they didn't love them anymore. Considering that women initiate divorce 70% of the time, this sort of thing is not uncommon. Diamonds might be forever, marriage on the other hand . . .

To be fair to women, the quality of men has declined as well. Men face roughly the same level of obesity, and plenty of men expect results while demonstrating little to no value in the dating market. The unemployed, obese, reddit moderator living in their parents' basement comes to mind. These are the "nice guys" that I mentioned back in Chapter 5. They believe that being agreeable is the only value that men need to display when seeking a woman.

However, like I said back in Chapter 5, this is due to comforting lies told by various parts of society. It is somewhat understandable to see young men's confusion when the nice guy myth doesn't meet reality. But it's not just the "nice guys" that face scrutiny. Nearly all men face some sort of scrutiny for some kind of patriarchy that is plaguing society—a patriarchy that is hell bent on oppressing women and keeping them down as second-class citizens. I have been a card-carrying man for about 30 years at this point, and my invitation to any patriarchy party must have been lost in the mail.

I won't get to attend those parties because it is not real, and that is a shame because I imagine there would be tons of bacon. The "patriarchy" that feminists are always talking about does not exist. Men and the "patriarchy" are simply a scapegoat for various groups of women to deny personal responsibility (more of this in later chapters).

Men are put in a hard situation. Men who do not achieve success are losers who will fail in the dating market. High achieving men are part of the patriarchy who exist merely to steal opportunities from women. And men who try to return to characteristics that made men tough and ready to take on the world will fall into the category of "toxic masculinity."

What's toxic masculinity? WebMD posted an article about "toxic masculinity." The article defines 'toxic masculinity' as "an attitude or set of social guidelines stereotypically associated with manliness that often have a negative impact on men, women, and society in general. The term "toxic masculinity" isn't meant to imply that the idea of masculinity in itself is inherently bad. Instead, it's meant to point out that certain behaviors and ways of thinking often associated with masculinity, from mental and physical toughness to sexism and homophobia, have a negative and often dangerous impact on the world."[117]

I found this article to have an oddly ironic twist. The article says that "toxic masculinity" is not implying masculinity is bad, but when you read about "toxic masculinity signs," almost everything in that section either attacks masculine qualities or frames reasonable behavior as toxic. Here are the "toxic masculinity signs."

"Need for control. Toxic masculinity encourages men to assert their power and dominance. We see this often in domestic relationships. The 2017 report "The Man Box" found that 34% of men in the U.S. believed they should always have the final say in their relationship, and 46% believed that men deserved to know where their girlfriend or wife is at all times."[117]

This one is laughable because there must be a leader in a relationship. Someone must have the final say. People deal with authority all the time. When you are at work, you can typically make your case to a boss as to why a procedure or policy should change. But your boss will have the final say on the matter at the end of the day, for better or for worse. Furthermore, what is wrong with a man wanting the authority and responsibility of leadership? Are women who seek leadership roles in relationships toxic? No. Then why is it considered "toxic" for men to have a desire to lead? There are men who desire more traditional relationships, and they will want to have the authority that comes with the responsibility of leadership.

As for the second part, I wonder what percentage of women want to know where their husbands or boyfriends are. And I am not knocking women for this. There's nothing wrong with wanting to know where your spouse is as long as the behavior doesn't cross into abuse through control. Honestly, it's more alarming if your significant other doesn't want to tell you what they are doing. The reason: It is safe to assume that if someone refuses to say what they are doing, they might be doing something wrong. Say a woman calls her boyfriend while he's out. She asks him, "What are you doing?"

He says, "Nothing."

She asks, "Who are you with?"

He replies, "Nobody."

She asks, "Where are you?"

He replies, "None of your business." Man or woman, that kind of behavior should be a red flag.

"Promiscuity. Toxic masculinity praises men for having multiple sexual partners while expressing disgust at women who do the same."[117]

I want to clarify at the beginning of this section. I am assuming that this portion of 'toxic masculinity' is talking about the total number of sexual partners a person has had over the course of their life. And that it is not about having multiple sexual partners while in a committed relationship such as marriage. Adultery is not something that should be celebrated, regardless of who is doing the cheating.

This may come as a surprise, but men and women have different mindsets when it comes to sex. The reason it is seen as an accomplishment for men to be able to have multiple sex partners is because he can meet the hypergamy requirements of multiple women. It is an accomplishment that the average man can't achieve. Research done in the book *Dataclysm*[24] showed that women viewed 80% of men as below average. This means that the average man is seen as unattractive to women.

While men have to work against female hypergamy, women are aided by the male sex drive. The average woman will get far more attention than the average man. And it is why women who don't show restraint can end up sleeping with many men. There was a woman in Australia who slept with over three hundred men . . . in a year.[138]

Also, look how men and women view low body counts. Men tend to place high value on female virgins, so much so that a Muslim would be willing to blow himself up in exchange for the promise of seventy-two virgins in heaven. Like I said back in Chapter 5, the reason men value women with low body counts is because it ensures paternity of their offspring. The women who were seen as less promiscuous were perceived by men to be less prone to infidelity and a safer long-term bet.

Now if you want to say that neither party should be praised for having a high number of sexual partners, that's a valid argument. But I doubt that the people who are enthralled by the sexual revolution will accept that argument. Doing so would imply that there is wisdom in the conservative restrictions of the sexual marketplace.

"Refusing to help with household duties. Toxic masculinity rejects roles traditionally considered "women's work." Toxically masculine men often refuse to participate in these household duties. "The Man Box" found that 22% of U.S. men believed they shouldn't have to do household chores 44% believed they should be the sole income earners, and 28% believed that boys shouldn't be taught things like cooking, cleaning, and child care."[117]

Again, this is something that attacks traditional gender roles. If a man is going to be the sole provider for the family and work eight to ten hours a day, its only reasonable that his spouse will support him by filling in the gaps, meaning that the house is clean, the kids are taken care of, and food is cooked. And I am not diminishing the traditional, feminine role; in fact, I would argue that it is equally as important as the role of the provider. A household will save thousands of dollars over the course of a year by not sending their kids to daycare. And it can save even more if a woman is able to cook food for the family rather than eat at a restaurant several times a week.

At the end of the day, housework is just more work. And plenty of women want to be stay-at-home moms and spend time with their kids. When my brother and his wife had their first baby, I could see the eagerness that my sister-in-law had to take care of my niece. (And she mothers the crap out of that little girl, too.)

But this traditional femininity is mocked and ridiculed in today's media. In 2022, a stay-at-home mom posted her routine on Facebook. The woman said that before she went to bed, the house was clean, and a load of laundry was going. She would also wake up with her husband at 4:30 a.m. to make him breakfast and coffee, and pack lunches for him and her kids. A group of news anchors brought attention to her post and shamed her for it. The TV chyron read "back to the 50s." The anchors were laughing at the woman and mocking her and her husband. All for the great crime of loving and supporting her family[150].

And the truth is that the 28% of men who believed that boys shouldn't be taught things like cooking, cleaning, and childcare are idiots. Those skills are not inherently feminine or masculine. It's just work that needs to be done, and it could offer some relief to their spouse.

"Risk-taking. Taking risks and suppressing fear is another feature of toxic masculinity. As a result, men are more likely to abuse drugs, drive dangerously, gamble, and engage in violence."[117]

Risk taking is a key aspect of masculinity. In the competition with other men for female attention, men will need to find a way to make themselves stand out from the rest. Risk-taking behavior is a direct result of female hypergamy. Men will drive fast and recklessly to impress women with their bravado. Men will take dangerous, higher paying jobs so that they can have the resources women desire. The best example of this is seen in male workplace fatalities. Even though men make up approximately half the workforce, men account for over 90% of workplace fatalities. Sometimes the risks pay off; sometimes they don't.[139]

"Stoicism. A cornerstone idea of toxic masculinity is that showing emotion is weak and feminine. Men are expected to be mentally and physically tough without breaking. Statistics and studies show that men are less likely to pursue mental health services like therapy despite being 1.8 times more likely than women to commit suicide."[117]

This one exposes the flaws in the concept of "toxic masculinity." Stoicism is apparently a cornerstone of toxic masculinity. But the article completely misrepresents the ideas of stoic philosophy. Stoicism is not about hiding your feelings; it is about having the ability to maintain self-control.

The key idea of stoicism is that there will be things in this world that you will be unable to control. Because you can't control these things, you should not waste time and effort trying to do so. Instead, focus on what you can control. You may not be able to control a situation, but you can control how you respond. And your response can make a big difference in how a series of events plays out.

One of the best examples of stoicism can be found in the movie *Flight* starring Denzel Washington. In the opening scene, he is a pilot on a commercial flight. While the plane is in mid-flight, the systems in the plane malfunction, and the plane begins to rapidly descend. In that instant, the stewardesses, the passengers, and the copilot start to panic. And the panic is reasonable; the plane is falling out of the sky at 30,000 feet.

But Washington doesn't panic. He commands the situation with stoicism. He instructs the flight crew to get the passengers to brace for impact. He calmly instructs his copilot to do various tasks to buy time. And he clearly communicates with air traffic control on the situation. Even though he could be moments away from death, he maintains his composure. He does not yell or panic. Why? Because everyone on that plane is counting on him to save them.

He couldn't control that the plane's systems were failing. But he could control his own actions. And because of that control, he was able to make an emergency landing in a field, preventing the deaths of the passengers.

"Violence. Toxic masculinity encourages men to use aggression and violence to assert their dominance and masculinity. "The Man Box" report found that 23% of U.S. men believed that if needed men should use violence to get respect."[117]

This is another misrepresented concept. Men do not need to be violent to display dominance and earn respect. We are social creatures; competence and social skills can easily help men exist in a social order. Bullies and tyrants won't make it very far in life if violence is all they have at their disposal. After all, I don't think one man can intimidate a group of five or six men.

While it is not necessary for all men to be violent, it is necessary for all men to have that capacity. Why? Because nature is violent.

Humans have simply gotten comfortable enough in modern society to forget this. Look at all the predators in nature. Tigers tearing open the necks of gazelles doesn't strike me as proof of love and peace in nature. Even our primate cousins, chimpanzees, commit violence among rival chimpanzee factions. And this isn't a small scuffle. Chimps will violently and ruthlessly tear other chimps apart.

Since men have often been the protectors of humanity, that ability to defend oneself and one's family is important. Violence will always be a part of nature. And there is nothing inherently wrong with violence. What matters is the context behind the actions. For example, I have five nieces. I can tell you that I would fight man or beast to keep them safe. I don't care if my own death occurs, I am willing to risk it for the people that I care about. And I am no different than the millions of men who would be violent to protect their loved ones—men who would fight like hell to protect their wives, children, friends, and family. Doesn't that change the circumstances of the situation? Or at the very least, add nuance to the situation?

That brings me back to the concept of toxic masculinity. There is nothing toxic about masculinity. There is only good behavior and bad behavior.

What feminists and WebMD fail to understand is that all masculinity comes from the same well. Some men will use their strength to hurt and bully others. I'm sure we all know someone who is like that, butut masculinity does more than harm. I knew a guy who was a volunteer firefighter. He told me that one night an apartment caught fire because somebody put a blanket over a space heater. He saved several people that night. He also went into that burning building multiple times so that he could recover several dead kids from the fire. And keep in mind, he was a volunteer firefighter and not getting paid to do that. It was a selfless and heroic act. I am not saying that women are incapable of these acts, but it is more likely that it comes from a man. In 2023, 5% of career firefighters were women. And 11% of the volunteer fire service are women.[118]

While both acts are different in their outcomes, they are drawn from the same masculine source. The reason for the difference in outcome has nothing to do with masculinity itself. Masculinity is neither good nor toxic. It is a variety of male traits and behaviors that have allowed men to survive.

Think of masculinity as a river. A river can flood your home, and kill you, your family, and your pets. It is a dangerous force of nature. And yet, civilizations throughout human history have chosen to build their societies near rivers. Why? Because the same river that can cause massive devastation can also be a positive force for civilization. While the risk of floods was always a possibility, people learned how to use rivers for their betterment. People used the river as a source of drinking water. They use the water for agriculture. And before roads were developed, rivers were used to transport goods between settlements. And people also learned to control the dangers. They didn't build their homes right on the river. They could also build dams or levees.

Consider the varied concepts of masculinity. Men have acted as brutal barbarians who raid and pillage the weak. Men also acted as the gallant defenders of their homes, protecting women and children from death or enslavement. Masculinity in and of itself is about as evil as a river.

In the *Sleeping Beauty* example, Phillip doesn't run up to the dragon, rip its heart out, and take a huge bite out of the dragon's heart. He is armed with truth and virtue. The truth and virtue temper his masculinity and act as a guide.

Toxic masculinity has become a description of anything that men do that women don't like, or use of the word generalizes a way in which men are different. What if a man is hesitant about marriage because of divorce laws and family court? Is he toxic? Maybe he just needs to man up and get married. Coincidently, pretty much anything "real men" do seems to benefit women.

But what happens when men do the right thing? What happens when men 'man up'? There is certainly no appreciation. I have heard that when 'bad' happens that adversely affects men, women are still seen as the victims. The best example of this comes from a Hillary Clinton quote: "Women have always been the primary victims of war. Women lose their husbands, their fathers, their sons in combat. Women often have to flee from the only homes they have ever known. Women are often the refugees from conflict and sometimes, more frequently in today's warfare, victims. Women are often left with the responsibility, alone, of raising the children."[35]

Yep. Men go off to war. Often for no better reason than because corrupt and cowardly politicians demanded war. The worst-case scenario is that men are killed. Others risk getting their limbs blown off and seeing their friends get killed. And if they survive, many suffer post-traumatic stress disorder. And I guess Hillary also didn't consider that it is equally painful for a father to have to bury his son. Or a son to see his father get buried.

Other quotations show that men are not being recognized. In a more recent attempt to pander to women, on the *Steve Harvey Show*, Steve Harvey said the following, "Marriage is not 50/50. It has never been 50/50. It will never be 50/50. I'm going to hold up a card and I'm going to show you what marriage is. Marriage is 85/15: 85 to the woman and 15 to the man. And let me explain something to you. The reason a woman is in charge of the house is because they know more about it. They know the kids' schedule, they know your schedule, they know the bills, they know where everybody goes. They take care of vacations; they run everything in the house because they care about everything. You a dude. You just know about your job; you don't know nothing else."[36]

It's crazy to hear this from a guy. But his audience is mostly women, so he has to pander to them. And all the women clapped and cheered at this.

Harvey says that men only account for 15% of the work in a marriage is because the only thing a man knows is his job. Even though men are expected to contribute more than their job, I'll act like that's all a man brings to the table. Well let me tell you about that job. (And I'm assuming that Steve is referring to traditional gender roles in his arguments.) That job is the reason why there is a house for a woman to oversee. That job is the reason why there is money to pay the bills. That job is the reason why the kids can have extracurricular activities. That job is the reason why the family gets to take those vacations. That job . . . even after all . . . that is only worth 15%?

I remember talking about something like this with a friend. I think we were talking about chivalry. I remember he told me, "You know I don't mind doing those things for women, but it would be nice to have someone show their appreciation." But society acts as though it does not need or appreciate men.

In 2023, Youtuber Shoe0nhead, did a video about the rise of male loneliness.[148] Shoe0nhead is a liberal who wanted to address the problem of male loneliness and then asked how the political left had failed men. When she talked about male loneliness, she referred to more than romantic relationships. It was also about men who had a lack of close personal friendships. In the video, she blames technology, social media, the mainstream media, low wages, and a lack of community.

Despite her being my political opposite, I appreciated her bringing some form of attention to the issue. And many other men did as well. Her comment section was filled with men that this video was likely talking about. Men who said how worthless they felt and that they just wanted someone to feel like they cared about them, and others discussed their suicidal ideations.

For simply talking about this issue Shoe0nhead, received backlash and hate from feminists. In a response video,[149] Shoe0nhead showed some of the responses. One of the comments read, "Men are subhuman and their loneliness can't be cured because they can't relate to actual human beings." Other women took pleasure in the suffering of young men saying, "you don't understand the pleasure it gives me to see these men crying and depressed. Imagine losing in a world that is literally built for you." And people wonder why men don't want to express their emotions.

The truth is that suffering is a part of every man's life. And it is something that men are sensitive to. It doesn't surprise me that Shoe0nhead also received backlash from some men. Men leveraged two lines of attack towards Shoe0nhead.

The first line of attack accused her of being a grifter and a chameleon. For those who don't know, a chameleon is a term used to describe a woman who makes content relating to men's struggles. She will pretend to be sympathetic towards men. But the chameleon doesn't really care about men; they only want to appeal to men, so that the chameleon can build a larger brand for themselves.

And it's not just women that try to exploit male loneliness to build their brands. Plenty of pick-up artists and communities say that they will help fix men . . . for a moderate fee. The "manosphere grifter" is a modern rebrand of the snake oil salesman. And this is something that men are rather sensitive to. This argument was a bad faith attack on Shoe0nhead. Her content covers a wide range of social issues, and she doesn't hide her liberal views. So, I don't see her making grifts that would appeal to traditional men, like the *trad* wife trend.

For those who don't know, the trad wife trend was a bunch of "traditional women" who would upload videos of themselves cooking and cleaning house while wearing makeup and a dress. It was a grift women used to create a brand for themselves including an online following by appealing to the desires of traditional conservatives. It was both sad and hilarious to see traditional conservatives fawn over amateur porn stars pretending to portray conservative values in the most over-the-top ways.

The second line of attack wasn't so much directed toward Shoe0nhead, as much as it was toward several shows. Shoe0nhead was invited on a few local shows to talk about the struggles of men. Having a woman talk about struggles related to masculinity rubbed some people the wrong way.

A good comparison would be if during the height of the #MeToo movement, a news panel invited a man to talk about sexual harassment and other unique challenges that women face in the workforce. Women would be insulted by having men represent such a personal issue that mostly affects women.

Naturally, some men were insulted by having a woman talk about the unique struggles that men face.

But I think Shoe0nhead was acting in good faith and trying to bring attention to the fact that men are struggling. And it does show something. The hero's journey for men isn't the same as it once was. Men were told to conquer the chaos of the world, and we would receive the admiration of others. Look at some of the classic tales such as *Beowulf*, a man who slays monsters and dragons. Or consider *The Odyssey,* where Odysseus wanders for ten years to return to his kingdom, son, and faithful wife.

Things have changed for men. We live in the age of instant gratification where one's "happiness" trumps any duty one may owe to others. The divorce rate is so high in America that the probability of a failed marriage is nearly a flip of a coin. And just because a marriage remains intact doesn't mean it's a happy marriage. If you want to see the chances of a happy marriage, read *The Book of Numbers* by Aaron Clarey.

Maybe you're a guy who really wanted to be the husband and father who had a loyal wife and loving kids to honor and cherish you until you go six feet in the dirt. That option may not be on the table anymore, but that does not mean that you need to take the Smith and Wesson retirement plan at age thirty.

You can work hard for *you.* Find a job or a skill that provides the resources to live a comfortable life. If you do not have to worry about providing for anyone else, living becomes a lot cheaper. You can buy an acre of land, a tiny home, and live a minimalist lifestyle. That will help you save money for retirement and any vacation you may want to take.

The government will inevitably try to take your money because the government has to give money to the parasites. But you can rebel against state governments by leaving states with high property and income taxes.

Once you are living comfortably, and you have spare time, spend that time making friends that genuinely care about you. Engage in hobbies that will bring you happiness. Take trips to places that you want to see before you die. Watch reruns of Maury Povich or Jerry Springer to fulfill your guilty pleasure for trash TV. Live your life for you and live it well.

And don't follow the path of bitter people who lash out at society. There's a saying, "Anger is the devil's cocaine." Sure, it might feel good to get riled and angry, but eventually that poisons your mind and spirit. You can still have a life worth living. It's like Inigo Montoya said in *The Princess Bride*: "There's not a lot of money in revenge."

# Reason 8: There's No Personal Accountability

"I never have a bad word to say about any of my four ex-wives. Because in each case, I gave them the key to the front door. It was my bad judgment that brought them into my life."

–Tom Leykis

When it comes to personal standards, people have two duties to fulfill. The first duty is to live the best life they can. This life is limited, and you only get one shot at it. So why throw it away on substance abuse and other terrible choices that will land you in poverty? Substance abuse can not only cause you to waste a high percentage of your disposable income (an even higher percentage if you are living in poverty), but it can also diminish your chances for future economic growth, especially if substance abuse interferes with your work. Unfortunately, a lot of people don't live up to the first expectation.

And because terrible decisions lead to hardship, society typically wants to help these people out. Unfortunately, this leads to a feedback loop where we end up with the subsidization of poor decision-making. The people that I refer to as "parasites" are those who make terrible decisions in their lives and refuse to hold themselves accountable for their mistakes. Instead, they rely on society to offer a bailout.

In an old John Stossel video from a few years ago,[113] he asked a panhandler if he was willing to work. The panhandler turned down nearly all the jobs that were offered to him. When Stossel found a job that was acceptable to the panhandler, the panhandler said that he wouldn't work five days a week. Why not? Because he didn't want to. His response was something along the lines of, "Why should a person have to work if they don't want to?" Fair enough. Every person should be given the choice to work or starve. That's fine if he doesn't want to work, so long as he doesn't mooch off other people. It would also be nice if he didn't vote in politicians who want to steal more of my money though taxes and redistribute it to lazy parasites. Unfortunately, that's exactly what people like him do. It's a shame that society tolerates this parasite leeching off others so that he can subsidize his own laziness.

You may be asking, "Why are you so unwilling to help people in need?" I'm not. I am against subsidizing poor decision-making. I am not knocking people who have genuinely fallen on hard times; in fact you, the reader, likely has suffered from hard times at one point or another. I have. Aaron Clarey, the man who wrote the foreword, faced poverty.

The difference between people on hard times and parasites is that parasitism is a permanent mindset. If you give a parasite a million dollars, within a decade, they will either be broke or dead.

I am also not knocking charitable people. Charity is one of the seven heavenly virtues after all. In Baton Rouge, there are signs that say, "DON'T GIVE MONEY TO PANHANDLERS. GIVE MONEY TO CHARITY INSTEAD." That way people who have fallen on hard times can get some of the resources that they need, and parasitic free riders are not given the economic incentive to ride free. The thing about charity is that it is meant to help people of a community get through hard times while they attempt to rebuild their lives, not to subsidize parasitism.

Parasitism is typically due to the lack of personal accountability. This lack of personal accountability can be seen in people's attempt at achieving some sort of victim status. After all, when you're a victim, nothing is ever your fault. There are even ideologies that are based on being a victim and the degree of which one is a victim. The best example of this is intersectionality.

Intersectionality: "the complex, cumulative way in which the effects of multiple forms of discrimination (such as racism, sexism, and classism) combine, overlap, or intersect especially in the experiences of marginalized individuals or groups."

A better definition is *the degree to which you can blame others for your shortcomings.* This can come in the form of blaming factors such as race, gender, class, etc. Give it a few years, and people who identify as cats will blame people how identify as dogs. And the best part is that while you are avoiding any sort of personal growth or development from your mistakes, other people will pay for your mistakes.

Lack of personal accountability isn't something that pertains to any specific age group, gender, race, sexual preference, etc. It is something that is facing nearly all groups in American society.

What's that? You're a boomer who didn't properly prepare for your retirement? Well, you are in luck. There are plenty of politicians that are eager to buy your vote. These politicians will take money from young people and redistribute it to you (if it's not obvious, I am talking about Social Security). Sure, you had over forty years to build and accumulate wealth. And yes, you could have gotten an annuity, personal retirement plan, or a life insurance policy. Certain life insurance policies build cash value over time that you can withdraw. You also could have taken that money and paid off debts so that when you retire, you have limited your fixed monthly expenses. But you did let the government take your money, so when you got old, you got to say that you, "paid into Social Security" even though you never had a choice.

Come again? You have over $50,000 in student loan debt? It's okay; your degree will help you get a high-paying career so you can pay back your loan. You majored in gender studies with a minor in communications? Well, I'm sure your experience partying with a bunch of dude-bros will help you. And I am noticing that the ROI on your "college experience" is probably somewhere between 0% and 0%. Oh, that's less than the interest on your subsidized student loans.

Well, how about a student loan bailout? Sure, no one forced you to go to college. You could have gone into the military first and used the GI bill to pay for school. That way your worthless degree wouldn't have you fifty grand in the hole. But it's okay. There are lots of people to help you with your bailout. They can pay more in taxes and inflation, all because you didn't bother to plan for when the student loan bill comes due.

A one-night stand got you pregnant because you didn't use any form of birth control? Don't worry; you should not be held accountable for your actions. We will solve this problem in the most rational and humane way. Let's go ahead and let doctors rip your unborn baby apart limb from limb in the womb. After all, it is not murder; it's health care.

Sure, the problem could have been avoided with basic planning and risk assessment. And sure, you are punishing your own child for the great crime of merely existing. It's like we learned back in Chapter 3, it's the duty of the child to pay for the mistakes of the parents. So, don't let your conscience bother you. You are empowered with the right to choose . . . to pass on your consequences to someone else.

The abdication of personal responsibility has become quite the racket today. People with victim mentalities have brought about new buzzwords. One of the more popular words that you will hear from journalists, politicians, and activists is "equity."

In a word, "equity" means "fairness." It typically involves rewarding productive people to ensure that productivity and morale remain high. Let's say you have two potential employees applying for a job. Person A is an employee with a better resume, work history, and education level than person B. Person A should likely get the job, but person B should also be allowed the opportunity to make the case as to why he or she should get the job. The true version of equity is equality through opportunity.

Over the last few years, the term "equity" has changed its meaning. Equity used to involve factors such as work ethic, education, work history, and merit. All these things are important. And what makes this definition of equity favorable is that each category can be improved by anyone. It just depends on what the individual is willing to do to improve and what sacrifices he or she is willing to make.

But today, the equity conversation revolves around sexual preference, race, and gender. It typically involves trying to secure more favorable outcomes for various intersectional groups. The problem with this definition of equity is that it is based on immutable characteristics. And it encourages discriminatory behavior to punish or reward people based on these traits.

A recent example of this is the Harvard admissions scandal. High performing Asian applicants were being negatively impacted by race-based admissions. As Kenny Xu of *City Journal* writes, "It has long been established that Asian-Americans and whites suffer disproportionately due to Harvard's race-based admissions, which have created an upswell of resentment from frustrated Asian and white college applicants. In his expert witness testimony, Duke University economist Peter Arcidiacono estimates that an Asian-American with a 25% chance of admission to Harvard would have a 33% chance if he or she were white, a 75% chance if Hispanic, and a 95% chance if black. Furthermore, the average Asian-American admittee to Harvard had SAT scores roughly 120 points higher than blacks admitted and 50 points higher than whites. (This is a low estimate, as a third or more of Asian applicants would have scored higher than the maximum SAT score had the maximum been increased.)"[146]

There is one other thing that proponents of "equity" don't think about. They see two people in the same field of work and observe that the salaries are different. These people will be quick to call out some type of discrimination, but there are other factors to control because before you can determine that discrimination is the cause of the disparity, you must control for geographic location, experience, job title, type of shift worked, number of hours worked, job market when hired, etc. Before you can even begin to have the discussion about discrimination, you must show that a significant portion of the market fits these criteria. I say greater than or equal to 5% because that puts the possible discrimination within two standard deviations.

This new type of "equity" is being promoted at different levels of American society. As a result, "diversity," "equity," and "inclusion" have become three popular buzzwords among left-wing journalists, politicians, and university administrators. Harvard has an office for equity, diversity, inclusion, and belonging. And these DEI programs don't come cheap. The University of Michigan paid more than thirty million dollars on its DEI program after one year. "Oklahoma's public universities spent $83.4 million on DEI over the last 10 years. Florida's public universities reported spending $34.5 million during the 2022-23 academic year. The University of Wisconsin was poised to spend $32 million over the next two years."[147] This has even made its way into the

White House. The U.S. President Joe Biden has given several speeches saying that creating "equity" was a priority for his administration.

This "equity" is being promoted because of people's perceived victimhood. I am not saying that conditions such as racial or gender discrimination did not have an impact in the past. However, I would argue that the United States is beyond these factors. Find me the corporate policy that meets the criteria for discrimination, and I will agree that something needs to change. But most negative outcomes in one's life are due to personal decision-making and not systemic oppression. A disparity in outcome does not mean that discrimination has taken place.

A common metaphor used by people who promote "equity" is to think of life as a race. A couple of years ago Channel 4 "Entertainment" did a video using this metaphor. A teacher lined up a group of students and told them they would be running a race, but the starting point for each student would be determined by the way they answered questions. Some of the instructions were "if English is your parents first language step forward. If you have ever been the only person in the room of your race, take a step backward. If you've never been asked 'where you come from' take a step forward.[34]

By the end of the video there were disparities between the students. And many of the students were either discouraged because they were further back or ashamed that they were in the front. These people see "equity" as a way for society to compensate for people not starting at the same point. But there are several problems with this line of thinking.

The biggest problem is that this metaphor does not account for factors such as individual drive, talent, and good decision-making. It automatically assumes that the people who start from behind will remain behind the pack permanently unless society intervenes.

Here is a final thought experiment. In this experiment, there are two people, person A and person B. Person A is a heterosexual white male; person B is a bisexual black female. Both people are willing to work and to avoid decisions that can land them in permanent poverty (substance abuse, having children out of wedlock, etc.). The critical distinction that I will put between the two is their fields of study. Person A gets a degree in marketing, Person B gets a degree in petroleum engineering. Who has a greater chance of success?

I would argue person B. Given the demand and salaries of petroleum engineers, it is highly likely that person B will be within the top 10% of income earners in the United States. Even though electric cars are popular right now, most Americans will rely on fossil fuels for decades to come.

The purpose of this example is to demonstrate that you can't control where you start. But you can control your effort and decisions in life. Someone who starts life poor or in a tough household can still make the most out of their life. It doesn't mean that it'll be easy. But if you work hard and work smart, you can rise in American society.

Hard work and good decision making are necessary, even if you start life in good circumstances. Starting life as a wealthy person does not guarantee success. The only thing wealth allows is more room for mistakes. But there are mistakes that no amount of money can save you from. I've always said, "Heroin will kill a rich person just as quick as a poor person."

# Reason 9: People Act Terribly Because They Know They Can Get Away With It

"Social media made y'all way too comfortable with disrespecting people and not getting punched in the face for it."

–Mike Tyson

I'm sure at some point or another you have seen a bratty child throwing a temper tantrum in a public setting. Why do they do that? It's because they know that they can get away with it. One of the best ways to instill proper behavior is to set rules and punishments for when those rules are broken.

What is "proper behavior"? In society, everyone must abide by an agreed set of rules. Although I fear authoritarianism, anarchy is not a viable substitute for authoritarianism. Anarchy simply creates a decentralized form of tyranny. Instead of being victimized by a single despot, people are victimized by mobs or gangs.

Proper behavior is adherence to laws passed by local officials, assuming that these laws are not violating a person's civil rights. One of the good things about the United States is that one can move from a place that does not reflect their values. And the results can be mixed. While you can be in a location that is more in line with your values, you may face different problems in different places. You can have vagrants crapping in the streets of San Francisco and LA or men walking around in public with AR-15s in Texas.

The instilling of proper behavior starts at home with parents. Sure, some parents act like complete tyrants and cross into the realm of child abuse. But there is a bigger problem than these parents. It is the parents who refuse to instill discipline and parents who never tell their kids "No." Kids may be innocent, but that does not mean they are good. When it comes to parents and their children, someone will end up being the boss of the other.

It is usually a much more stable situation when the parent is in charge. When the child is in charge, it will be a house of chaos. I remember listening to a radio advertisement with my brother Mark when we were riding to school together. The ad was about kids with behavioral issues. The ad featured a mother saying, "I'll never forget the day my son yelled he hated me at the top of his lungs, and then slammed the door in my face."

I thought about it for a second and started laughing. I asked Mark, "Do you have any idea what Dad would have done to us if we did that? Dad would have kicked down the door, whooped our ass, and then make us fix the door." We both got a pretty good laugh out of that.

But too many parents refuse to discipline their children. And this is not a left versus right issue. There are parents on both sides who are too concerned with being liked by their children. They look at my father's approach and say, "Oh my gosh. That is so barbaric, I could never do that." But parents don't have to go to such extremes. A simple "no" or timeout is a good start. All parents need to do is establish rules and use negative reinforcement to punish bad behavior. By not establishing these rules and expected behaviors, parents risk raising brats for children who are prone to temper tantrums.

The problem with these bratty kids is that they grow up and become entitled adults. And they will often do things to other people and expect to get away with it. One of the best examples of this was during the BLM riots of 2020. There was a video of a young white woman yelling at police officers. She was probably some suburbanite princess who had never heard the word "no." She was yelling at a group of cops and getting in cops' faces. The cops warned her to get back. She yelled, "or what?" The cops warned her again to get back. Then she got even closer and yelled, "*Or fucking what?*"

Well, she found out right then and there. Not two seconds after she yelled at the cops, they grabbed her, brought her to the ground, and arrested her. The entire time the cops were arresting her, she was screaming bloody murder. She really did not expect the cops to do anything. I don't know if she thought she had white privilege or some other societal privilege, but for what was probably the first time in her life, she had to face the consequences of her actions.

This is not just a left-wing issue. The January 6, 2021 U.S. Capitol riot is proof of this. A bunch of angry conservatives rioted, attacked police, and vandalized government property. They did this because they believed that Donald Trump won the election and that the election had been stolen. No doubt every one of these rioters complained about the BLM riots months before. Yet their respect for law enforcement and public property mysteriously vanished.

To make matters worse, these rioters stormed the Capitol building and delayed the confirmation of a new president. An unprecedented act. Was our republic close to being extinguished? No. These people had no institutional support and were not capable of starting a new government even if they had support. The rioters were too stupid to follow Donald Trump's instructions to "peacefully and patriotically make your voices heard."

Then you have people who are just plain stupid and inconsiderate. This is common among environmental activists. There are photos and videos of activists blocking traffic or trying to damage historical art. The environmental activists will sit in the street and not even move if vehicles are trying to get through. The activists are treated like a bunch of small children even though most of them are young adults. And there is the occasional boomer left over from the hippie era. In some cases, drivers will get out of their vehicles and drag protesters off the road. And once the protester is dragged to the side of the road so people can get through, the protestor gets up, and runs back to sit in the street.

In 2022, a group of eco protesters glued their hands to the floor of a Volkswagen Museum. The protesters refused to remove the glue and leave. There is a funny twist to the story. The museum staff simply turned off the lights and left the building, leaving the protesters in the dark, without the ability to order food or go to a restroom. The protesters were upset that their needs were not accommodated by Volkswagen.

Aside from the bad behavior, all these things have something in common. If done correctly, these things could have been legal in the United States. The

BLM protests/riots happened across the country in the summer of 2020. I found that BLM's claims of systemic discrimination and widespread murder of black Americans at the hands of police to be lacking evidence.

For starters, black people being shot by the police is not a widespread epidemic. The *Washington Post* keeps an interactive database of people killed by the police.[135] According to the *Washington Post,* approximately 1,000 people are shot and killed by police each year. Black Americans make up around 25% of the people killed in shootings. That means around 250 black Americans are shot by the police per year. There are over forty million black Americans living in the United States today. The probability of a black American being shot by police in America is approximately 1 in 160,000 in a year. For reference, a person over the course of their lifetime has a 1 in 15,300 chance of getting struck by lightning.

The *Washington Post* suggests that black Americans are shot at a disproportionate rate because they constitute only 14% of the population. This would be disproportionate if encounters with the police were by random chance. However, police encounters are due to crime being committed. Criminals commit crimes, and the police respond. Because of this, crime rates are a better indicator of proportionality. According to 2018 FBI crime statistics,[137] black Americans were responsible for 27% of all crime in the United States, which correlates more accurately with the percentage of black Americans shot by the police.

Typically, when a suspect is shot by police, it is because the suspect presented danger to police. Over 80% of the black suspects who were shot were armed. And many of the people that were unarmed could still have assaulted the officers. For a most recent example, watch the dashcam footage of the shooting of Lenard Cure.[136]

You can see why I disagreed with the activists, but these people had the right to protest, and not every event turned into a riot. You can find many cases of the protests being peaceful and not "mostly peaceful."

The problem is when these protests turned into riots that caused billions of dollars in property damage. And these people were likely emboldened by politicians. During the riots, then vice presidential candidate Kamala Harris encouraged donations to the Minnesota Freedom Fund to bail out rioters. Saying of Facebook and Twitter, "If you're able to, chip in now to the @MNFreedomFund to help post bail for those protesting on the ground in Minnesota."[114]

The same is true for the January 6 Capitol riot. The conservative Trump supporters could have protested the election results. After all, every four years, there are millions of angry voters in America. So, it's not like that is far outside the realm of American politics. But they took it to a different level when they stormed the Capitol. I don't know if they thought Trump was going to protect them, but they clearly thought they were going to get away with it.

The thought of acting with impunity is not just seen in American politics; it has bled over into the culture. The thought of getting away with everything is why Karens exist. For those who don't know, a Karen is a woman who acts out her entitlement in public. The stereotypical Karen is typically white and middle aged, but I have heard the term Karen being used for women of various ages and races. Karens are not unique to one political side or the other. I have seen videos of racist Karens harassing Hispanics and Asian Americans. I have also seen videos of Karens harassing teenagers who were painting over BLM graffiti. That's right dear reader, Karenhood has transcended American politics.

Karens will usually engage in harassment or cause a scene. They go after people that they believe won't retaliate. There's a reason why they tend to go after retail and food service workers. They believe that since "the customer is always right," that means they can do whatever they want. And when they don't get exactly what they want, you had better be ready to get the manager.

And if you want to see perfect examples of people acting terribly because they can get away with it, watch protesters at college conservative events. These activists will try to disrupt the event, or even get the event shut down. I was a member of Turning Point USA at LSU. We held a campus clash event in 2019. Of course, there was no violence. Political commentators Charlie Kirk, Dave Rubin, and Candace Owens came to speak at our auditorium. Protesters disrupted the event and tried to stop the three hosts from speaking, even though there was a Q&A portion of the event. And if you disagreed with the speakers on anything, you were able to go to the front of the line to ask questions. If the protesters had something to say, they could have waited until that segment.

After seeing this, I usually wonder how much of this could have been avoided if parents disciplined their kids. It's better for children to learn discipline from their parents than from an outside source because the parents are typically a lot easier on their children than a judge or some stranger that they have pushed too far.

Take Charles Barkley for example. For those unfamiliar with Charles Barkley, he was a power forward in the NBA. He was 6'6" tall and weighed over 250 pounds. In 1997, a young man had the bright idea of throwing ice on Charles Barkley. How did Barkley respond to having ice thrown on him? He took the young man and threw him through a window. There are a lot of lessons you can learn from this; the biggest one is: Don't throw ice on Charles Barkley. Another lesson is: Don't mess with people. Granted, most people won't be dumb enough to pick a fight with a professional athlete, but there is always danger involved with trying to push people around. Eventually, you will screw with the wrong person.

Here's the thing about getting punched in the face: It hurts. People don't always have to get punched in the face to stay in line. If people understand that there will be consequences for their actions, it's usually enough to deter bad behavior. But today, too many people are emboldened by a lack of potential consequences.

This is the basis of Heather MacDonald's book, *The War on Cops*. In the book, MacDonald says that soft-on-crime policies mixed with anti-police attitudes leads to increase in crime. She notes what she calls a "Ferguson Effect," named after Ferguson, Missouri where Michael Brown was killed in 2014. The Ferguson Effect is the increase in crime that results in police being reluctant to enforce the law due to political pressure.

I want to be clear; I am not suggesting that society should have blind loyalty and fealty to law enforcement. If citizens and government officials want to hold law enforcement accountable, it is reasonable to outfit all vehicles with dashcams and all officers with body cams along with making the videos available to the public. These videos and information will defuse a lot of the tension between the public and law enforcement. But I don't support the dismantling of law enforcement.

I mentioned BLM and other groups in my previous book, *A Mostly Peaceful Book*. In 2020, crowds of people protested and demanded that police be defunded. What happened when cities agreed to this? You would see massive increases in crime. Cities like Minneapolis gave warnings to citizens about car jackings. The Minneapolis PD literally released a memo to citizens saying, "Be prepared to give up your cell phone and purse/wallet."[117] In New York City, small children were being killed by stray bullets. In San Francisco, many people take their valuables out of their car. Then they will leave their car doors open, their windows down, and trunks open. This is so that thieves will not smash their car windows in an effort to steal something valuable.[116]

You had people who would defend rioters as peaceful protesters. There was even a book published called *In Defense of Looting*: *A Riotous History of Uncivil Action*. But what happens when businesses operating with low profit margins are looted? They take their insurance money, and walk away. Then the communities lose jobs and places to shop.

In his book *Dismantling America* Thomas Sowell discusses the repercussions that things such as crime, shoplifting, rioting, and looting can have on neighborhoods. He says that in the 1940s, the Harlem neighborhood where he grew up had a wide variety of stores. The goods were good quality and prices were competitive. Unfortunately, "ghettos riots" as Sowell calls them, in the 1960s resulted in these stores being looted and burned. And these stores did not reopen. What few stores remained in these neighborhoods stocked fewer goods at higher costs and lower quality.

Similar results will likely be seen because of the 2020 riots. Looted businesses that were uninsured or underinsured are unlikely to reopen. And there were probably increases in insurance premiums for stores that were properly insured, which led to increases in the cost of doing business. All this was because American cities were unwilling to prevent and punish bad behavior.

The protagonist from the show *Mr Inbetween* had good insight on this. The protagonist of the show is a criminal named Ray. In one of the episodes, Ray beats up a couple of arrogant street punks. Ray then must go to court-mandated anger management group therapy sessions. In one of the sessions, the therapist is trying to get Ray to admit that what he did was wrong or get Ray to show remorse. But Ray is steadfast in his belief that he did nothing wrong.

The end of the exchange goes like this. The therapist asks, "Do you enjoy hitting people?"

Ray responds, "I wouldn't say I enjoy hitting people. If I hit someone, I generally got a pretty good reason."

The therapist asks, "And you think you had a good reason?"

Ray asks, "Didn't I just say that?" Getting visibly annoyed, the therapist asks Ray his reason for attacking the punks. Ray states, "Well, they were being assholes."

The therapist says, "The world is full of assholes Ray. You do realize that?"

Ray says, "Yeah and you know why?"

The therapist asks, "Why?"

And with a twisted smile on his face, Ray says, "Because people let them get away with it."

# Reason 10: People Are Narcissistic

"If you live your life as if everything is about you, you will be left with just that. Just you."

—Unknown

It is hard to say exactly what has led to the all-pervasive sense of narcissism on display in our society. My favorite theory blames the focus on childhood self-esteem rather than on personal achievement. To be fair, there is a correlation between success and confidence/self-esteem. The idea is that if you build confidence in someone, they will probably be more successful. The idea of boosting someone's confidence so they will be more likely to succeed is not absurd.

The problem is that success comes from competence, not confidence. People become more confident when they are successful. When the focus is on building new talents, people will learn the skills and work ethic necessary to succeed. This is true even if the person fails to meet a goal or expectation. Even when you come up short, you can take that loss and learn from your mistakes and further your improvement.

If you ever watch *The Last Dance* documentary that features Michael Jordan's basketball career, you can see how Michael Jordan used the pain and frustration of losing to drive him to be better. At several points in his career, Jordan and the Chicago Bulls came up short. One of the best examples of this is the Chicago Bulls' and Detroit Pistons' rivalry. In the

1990 playoffs, Detroit eliminated the Chicago Bulls from the playoffs. During the subsequent offseason, Jordan and the Bulls immediately started training again. Michael Jordan even put on fifteen pounds of lean muscle. They took the pain of losing to Detroit and used that to make themselves better. And Chicago won the NBA Championship in 1991. By focusing on developing talent, Chicago created champions.

But by focusing on self-esteem, you simply end up with entitled mediocre people. And when these entitled people do not get what they feel they deserve, they will typically play the victim in some way. A common theme that you may see throughout the chapter is that many of the groups I mention will try to identify as victims in American society. This chapter will reflect on some of the previous chapters and show the narcissism of some groups and movements. It is worth noting that not every group I mention is necessarily narcissistic. But they do show some narcissistic tendencies. I will begin each section with a quote from helpguide.org[29] that explains a narcissistic trait and then finds a group that embodies the trait.

"Needs constant praise and admiration—A narcissist's sense of superiority is like a balloon that gradually loses air without a steady stream of applause and recognition to keep it inflated. The occasional compliment is not enough. Narcissists need constant food for their ego, so they surround themselves with people who are willing to cater to their obsessive craving for affirmation . . . And if there is ever an interruption or diminishment in the admirer's attention and praise, the narcissist treats it as a betrayal."[29]

I have already talked about the LGBTQ+ movement and its authoritarianism. I already talked about how the movement tries to impose its will on people who do not agree with them. But that's not where the narcissism comes into play. There are people who demand constant attention and validation. And there are people who will base their entire state of being around the LGBTQ+ movement so that they can garner praise and attention.

When I was growing up in the late 1990s and early 2000s, the catchword was "tolerance." It essentially meant don't be a jerk to people who are different than you. If you don't like something, leave it alone. Fair enough. When I was in high school, most of the gay movement was focused on making gay marriage a right. It may not be something that I completely agree with, but there is a compelling argument for equal protection under the law. A brief breakdown of the argument goes like this: Since marriage is something that is offered and recognized by the government, the government cannot discriminate regarding whom it offers marriage to due to the protections of the Fourteenth Amendment. If the government does not recognize marriage, then it must offer a substitute with all of the perks and incentives offered in marriage. My overall attitude to gay people wanting to get married is akin to radio host Tom Leykis's opinion on the matter: "Be careful what you wish for."

However, the movement has changed over the last decade. While it used to be gays and lesbians pushing for tolerance, now a coalition of many groups demand societal praise for their behavior. Today it has gone well and above the push for tolerance and equality. After all, what rights do straight people have in 2024 that gay people don't have?

And the population of the LGBTQ+ movement has changed as well. It can range from transgender men demanding that society recognize them as women. It can be some people who call themselves "nonbinary" and demand that people use terms like "they" or "zim" when referring to them. A lot of it is simply a cry for attention. Nothing screams, "Please pay attention to me" more than the modern-day movement.

I would argue that anyone who tries to identify as non-binary is simply looking for attention. There are no requirements or barriers to entry; anyone and everyone can do it. Gay people must at least be attracted to the same sex. Even trans people tend to put some skin in the game by taking artificial hormones that can negatively impact their bodies. But when it comes to being "nonbinary," a person does not have to change his or her behavior in any way.

Demi Lovato said that she was nonbinary in 2021. Lovato wanted to use they/them pronouns. But then in 2022, she started using she/her pronouns. This nonbinary thing can pretty much change to anything at any time and yet these people demand that society cater to them.

And the movement gets corporate attention. Some corporations run marketing campaigns that pander to these groups. This is certainly true in the holy pride month in June. I remember a commercial from a few years ago. An Asian American wrote a speech for his family. He was planning to come out as gay to his family at what seemed to be a family reunion. It was a couple of minutes long, filled with dramatic music and tense scenes. There was no product placement, so you had no idea what the ad was for. And when you got to the end . . . it was an Oreo commercial! That came out of left field. Some pretty good memes came out of this. One meme had two marketing executives talking about the commercial. One said, "How does this commercial help us sell cookies?" The other executive replies, "Cookies?"

Mainstream media outlets write articles about how stunningly brave these people are. As I mentioned back in Chapter 4, Disney has targeted children with a "not-so-secret gay agenda." And of course, you have politicians who are eager to kiss ass and virtue signal. In 2022, then Speaker of the House Nancy Pelosi went on RuPaul's Drag Race. She said, "Your freedom of expression of yourselves in drag is what America is all about."[102]

And that's only what you see in the wider culture. On a more micro level, these groups start to seek attention from children. This can range from teachers using fictitious pronouns and forcing them on students, or drag queens performing inappropriate acts in front of groups of captive kids, who were forced to attend by parents or school officials.

A school in Lancaster, Pennsylvania, hosted a drag event for students without parents' permission in 2022. "The school's Gender Sexuality Alliance (GSA) club held the show after hours, hosting drag queens by the names of "Majestee," "Enigma," and "Hexxa." Meredith Hilt, a parent in the school district was shocked and appalled by the dancer's outfits, which "exposed butt cheeks and tight leotards with visible bulges." In an email, the teachers encouraged students to bring money to "tip the queens" and support the dancer's Instagram accounts."[103]

Plenty of people in the gay community simply want to live their lives in peace. I can respect that. But many others are seeking attention and validation. These people do not demand tolerance; they demand reverence. And if you do not grant them that attention, you will be branded a bigot of some kind. Which wouldn't be so bad if being called a bigot by some idiot online was the worst thing that can happen. Chaya Raichik, the woman in charge of "the libs of tiktok" account, was doxed. It's one thing to be called bad names. It is another thing for you to be open to threats and harassment in your personal life.

"Lives in a fantasy world that supports their delusions of grandeur- Since reality doesn't support their grandiose view of themselves, narcissists live in a fantasy world propped up by distortion, self-deception, and magical thinking. They spin self-glorifying fantasies of unlimited success, power, brilliance, attractiveness, and ideal love that make them feel special and in control. These fantasies protect them from feelings of inner emptiness and shame, so facts and opinions that contradict them are ignored or rationalized away."[29]

You could apply this description to several groups. You can definitely apply this to various social media influencers, but the group that I believe this applies to most is "fat acceptance" groups. Fat acceptance activists have nearly all the traits listed above. I do want to clarify that not all fat people belong in this category. Plenty of people dealing with obesity just want to live their lives in peace. They don't seek to push some form of social change on the rest of society because of their condition. I have nothing against people who are just trying to live their lives. The problem is with fat activists who try to claim victimization and rewrite societal standards because they are too lazy to lose weight.

The fantasy world that they live in is one where "big is beautiful," but it's not true. This is a lie that is told by fat activists for fat activists. "Big is beautiful" is not about beauty; it is about coping with one's lack of beauty. Most people do not have a burning desire to see people who are obese or morbidly obese. If obese people were as attractive as fit people, then there would not be a need for activism. There would already be a natural desire for obese people, and the problem would not exist.

It is worth mentioning what classifies as obesity. The CDC classifies obesity as results of a Body Mass Index or BMI. "If your BMI is less than 18.5, it falls within the underweight range. If your BMI is 18.5 to <25, it falls within the healthy weight range. If your BMI is 25.0 to <30, it falls within the overweight range. If your BMI is 30.0 or higher, it falls within the obesity range. Obesity is frequently subdivided into categories: Class 1: BMI of 30 to < 35 Class 2: BMI of 35 to < 40 Class 3: BMI of 40 or higher. Class 3 obesity is sometimes categorized as "severe" obesity"[105].

A study published by the National Library of Medicine showed that there was not a natural attraction toward obese people.[104] The study was performed across multiple cultures and regions. The countries in the study included China, Iran, Mauritius, Kenya, Morocco, Nigeria, Senegal, Austria, Lithuania, and the UK. The study measured the mean desired BMI for both male and female for all countries—except for Iran (mean desired BMI of 27 in females and 26.4 in males); all other countries mean desired BMI was in the healthy BMI range (18.5-24.9). And the Iranian-desired BMI did not fall in the obese category; it fell in the overweight category.

Furthermore, most of the countries allowed for at least one standard deviation from the mean without reaching obesity. For example, the UK had a desired mean female BMI of 22.6 with a standard deviation of ± 3.9, meaning that 68% of the values fall within the range of 18.7 to 26.5.

And this does not make fat people victims. Throughout human history, being overweight was a sign of privilege, status, and nobility. It meant that you could afford enough food to have a caloric surplus. Dying of starvation was far more prevalent than dying from obesity. Think of King Henry the Eighth of England. He was well known for his love of food and uxoricide. He was sought after by many women, but it was because he was the King of England, not because he was fat. Not only did he have high status in his society, but his wife and kids did not have to worry about starvation. However, the wife did run the risk of losing her head.

I have heard people talk about obesity as if it is a disease. You could say that it is a human condition, but not a disease. You can't catch obesity like the flu. You aren't going to go home, go to sleep, and wake up a hundred pounds heavier. Becoming obese is something that is done and maintained over the course of years. Obesity is a lifestyle that many people accept, even though there are ways to avoid it.

Keeping and maintaining a healthy long-term lifestyle is a way to lose weight and keep it off. It's not easy. This is especially true in America, home of Burger King, which is the home of the Whopper. If it were easy, everyone would do it. For those interested in a healthy diet, here are a couple of dietary recommendations from the CDC when trying to achieve a healthy diet. "Emphasizes fruits, vegetables, whole grains, and fat-free or low-fat milk and milk products. Includes a variety of protein foods such as seafood, lean meats and poultry, eggs, legumes (beans and peas), soy products, nuts, and seeds. Is low in added sugars, sodium, saturated fats, trans fats, and cholesterol. Stays within your daily calorie needs."[107]

But fat activists treat this advice like a snail treats salt. They will say that they are perfectly fine the way they are, and that we should see them as they see themselves. And what happens when fat activists see prominent fat people lose weight? They get furious. I remember actress Rebel Wilson took a lot of heat from fat activists because she decided to lose seventy-five pounds.[106] Singer Adele also drew criticism when she lost weight.[106]

This shows real selfishness among these fat activists. They act like crabs in a bucket. And this is downright evil when you consider the health ramifications of obesity. The CDC lists the following health effects associated with obesity. "People who have overweight or obesity, compared to those with healthy weight, are at increased risk for many serious diseases and health conditions. These include: all causes of death (mortality). High blood pressure (hypertension). High LDL cholesterol, low HDL cholesterol, or high levels of triglycerides (dyslipidemia). Type 2 diabetes. Coronary heart disease. Stroke. Gallbladder disease. Osteoarthritis (a breakdown of cartilage and bone within a joint). Sleep apnea and breathing problems. Many types of cancer. Low quality of life. Mental illness such as clinical depression, anxiety, and other mental disorders. Body pain and difficulty with physical functioning."[108]

"Exploits others without guilt or shame- Narcissists never develop the ability to identify with the feelings of others—to put themselves in other people's shoes. In other words, they lack empathy. In many ways, they view the people in their lives as objects—there to serve their needs. As a consequence, they don't think twice about taking advantage of others to achieve their own ends"[29].

I think very few groups should be considered true victims in our society. Usually, to count as being victimized, someone would have to experience something extremely harmful and out of their control. I consider women who have been raped as victims. I consider children who have been abused by their parents to be victims. And I consider many young transgender people to be victims.

I do want to clarify which transgender people I see as victims. I am not talking about the twenty-five-year-old who wanted to have a sex change operation. I am talking about children who have had gender dysphoria pushed on them by various groups and institutions in our society. Many of these groups exploit these people for different reasons.

I have already mentioned the Munchausen by Proxy" parents. These are parents who are willing to destroy the minds and bodies of their children for personal reasons. Typically, it is for social validation.

In a Timcast interview,[30] Jeff Younger is the father in a popular child custody case because his wife claims that one of his sons is transgender. In the interview, Mr. Younger said that his son did not present himself as a girl to anyone but his mother. And his son told a court-appointed psychologist, "Mommy doesn't love me if I'm not a girl." Mr. Younger still did not get full custody of his son. This example shows that the court system is more than willing to overlook child abuse as long as it suits an agenda.

This child abuse does not end at Munchausen by Proxy parents. Narcissistic teachers who are seeking to affirm their own beliefs are more than willing to indoctrinate children into this ideology. These teachers are more than willing to create gender and sexual confusion among children so that they can make themselves feel validated.

In my previous book (*A Mostly Peaceful Book: A Refutation of the Leftist Culture That Plagued* 2020), I mentioned that schools were indoctrinating children, but I was wrong about one thing. I wrote the book in 2020. Teachers were pushing diluted forms of critical race theory, usually through books like *Anti Racist Baby* by Ibram Kendi and Ashley Lukashevsky. I expected this to keep going, but this subject lost steam about a year later. While it likely still happens, it's not the primary subject anymore. To my surprise, teachers have started pushing LGBTQ propaganda on kids. I didn't think that people would be foolish enough to push sexual themes on kids, but propaganda comes in many forms, ranging from books, posters, teachers, and administrators.

In 2023, a New York school district faced a lawsuit from two parents who claimed that a teacher indoctrinated their child into becoming transgender. And the child began having suicidal ideations as a result of the confusion. The suit claimed, "[The teacher] pursued her own agenda outside the curriculum, which included persuading her 5$^{th}$ grade students to try 'being gay' or being another gender even when they were not. To further her agenda, [the teacher] read and provided her students graphic books about gender and sexuality which were not on the curriculum."[31]

But it still doesn't end there. It is with great shame and fury that I say that voices in the medical field are now pushing this bullshit on kids. I figured if anyone would be objective and try to stop this madness, it would be doctors. When I worked at Ochsner Health Systems, part of our motto was "patients first," giving high-quality patient care and ensuring positive long-term treatment.

I thought that this sense of care and duty would be evident at any hospital. But I guess I was young and naive. Hospital systems across the country cater to these children with gender confusion. These doctors will give puberty blockers to small children and they will perform mastectomies on teenage girls. I'd say these doctors fit the description of narcissistic sociopaths, "Narcissistic sociopaths seek to ingratiate themselves with power, money, pleasure, and other niceties and do so at the expense of others. They might lie, cheat, steal, and manipulate to get their way, and disregard other people's feelings, needs, wants, and even safety to achieve their goals"[145] (Mentalhealth.com).

In 2023, a whistleblower that worked at the Washington University Transgender Center at St. Louis Children's Hospital wrote a report for the *Free Press*. (Author's note: this article shows the depravity and disgust of these acts on children and other vulnerable people. While I may sum up the article, I encourage you to read it in its entirety. It will be number 32 in the works cited page, or you can Google "The Free Press Jamie Reed" and click on the link that says, "I Thought I Was Saving Trans Kids. Now I'm Blowing the Whistle.") In the report, the whistleblower mentions what should be considered malpractice by the Transgender Center.

The center served mostly teenagers that were mostly girls. The whistleblower predicts that 70% of their clients were teenage girls. But the patients did not just suffer from gender dysphoria; patients also suffered from eating disorders, depression, and anxiety. The center also accepted patients that were sent from mental health facilities. Some of these patients were suffering from schizophrenia, PTSD, and bipolar disorder. Many children had experienced abuse and neglect from their parents.

It was quite easy for these kids to be started on the path to transition. The report states that for girls to get testosterone, they only needed a letter of approval from a therapist. The therapist was usually recommended by the center and was often approved. The next stop was to an endocrinologist to fill the prescription for testosterone. Many of these girls likely did not understand the full weight of what they were doing. Throughout the report, the author lists multiple cases where children were given testosterone or puberty blockers. Below is an excerpt from the report.

"One of the saddest cases of detransition I witnessed was a teenage girl, who, like so many of our patients, came from an unstable family, was in an uncertain living situation, and had a history of drug use. The overwhelming majority of our patients are white, but this girl was black. She was put on hormones at the center when she was around 16. When she was 18, she went in for a double mastectomy, what's known as 'top surgery.' Three months later she called the surgeon's office to say she was going back to her birth name and that her pronouns were she and her. Heartbreakingly, she told the nurse, 'I want my breasts back.' The surgeon's office contacted our office because they didn't know what to say to this girl."[32]

You are probably reading this and wondering how these people could do that to kids—and extremely vulnerable ones at that. If so, that's a good thing. It shows that you are a decent person who has a sense of compassion for others. I adore a child's innocence. When I see a child, my first instinct is to preserve that child's innocence and keep the child safe. But these doctors and therapists see something else. They see an opportunity to exploit these kids and profit from their exploitation.

Why do it? It's simple. These facilities are willing to destroy kids' future for money. Dr. Shayne Sebold Taylor at Vanderbilt University Medical Center's was caught on video talking about all the benefits of the treatments. Taylor said that, "these surgeries make a lot of money. Female to male chest reconstruction can bring in $40,000. A patient just on routine hormone treatment, who I'm only seeing a few times a year, can bring in several thousand dollars."[33] She goes on to estimate that a female-to-male bottom surgery can bring in up to $100,000 per patient. Usually when somebody is talking about performing new forms of treatment, they tend to mention long-term outcomes. Usually, the best-selling point is that the patient will have a higher quality of life as a result of the treatments. But no, these doctors cite financial gain as their reasons for wanting to do these surgeries.

These people do not deserve to hold the title of "doctor." Their actions are a disgrace to the medical community. A doctor that provides good health care ensures that patients have multiple options in their health care and that the patient has positive long-term outcomes.

My oncologist friend that I mentioned back in Chapter 1 is an example of a great doctor. He did more than just treat the patient; he did what he could to raise the morale of the person he was treating. He took short- and long-term factors into consideration. He had in-depth conversations with patients about their treatment options. And he always ensured that his patients had an excellent understanding of what effects would come from treatment. Dr. Raj and any physician with an ounce of integrity would scoff at this medical malpractice.

Unfortunately, there is nothing that honorable physicians can do about this situation. This is especially true if upper management implements policy that mandates people be referred to these gender clinics. Despite these revelations, activists continue to push gender-affirming health care. And politicians are more than willing to subject these children to the horrors that come with chemical castration and genital mutilation.

This is why I said that I consider young trans people to be victims. These people have no one to help them out of their situation. They face indoctrination from so many sources. There are parents whose job it is to protect and guide their children. And yet they would rather destroy any chance their child has at a normal life so they can get some likes on social media.

The doctors and therapists won't care either. They simply care about getting their money and nothing else. It doesn't matter what kind of damage they cause to the patient. What makes this so unforgivable, is that these are people who know better. They know the side effects of the medicines that they give. They know that the surgeries can cause irreversible damage to the patient's body. They know that they are trusted by the public. Then they take that trust, throw it in the garbage, and inject children with misery.

# Final Thoughts

Even though I am a capitalist at heart, there are instances where capitalism in and of itself is not the only thing that makes a society prosperous. Capitalism can lead to great material abundance, job freedom, and innovation. But capitalism does not pick and choose which demand to offer a supply for. Capitalism can be a force for prosperity in the world. Capitalism, however, can lead to evils like chemical castration and genital mutilation of children, AKA gender-affirming care. Capitalism won't work unless there is a moral and spiritual element working along with it.

The same lack of morals from physicians that engage in gender-affirming care is seen in different levels of our society. The legacy media is a prime example of this. Journalists will throw away journalistic integrity to push a partisan political narrative.

The coverage of the death of Philando Castile in 2016 is one story that the mainstream media tried to spin in a way that would get them the highest ratings. Philando Castile was shot by police during a traffic stop in Falcon Heights, Minnesota. Castile was pulled over for a broken taillight. He was with his girlfriend and her four-year-old daughter. Castile had a pistol. It was a legal gun, and he had a permit to carry the gun. When the officer arrived at the driver's-side window, Castile informed the officer that he had a gun on him. The cop told him not to reach for the gun. Castile said that he wasn't reaching for it. The officer and Castile were both nervous at that point. In the confusion, the cop fired multiple shots, killing Castile.

Looking back at the evidence and the story, the shooting was not justifiable. If Castile was planning to shoot the officer, he wouldn't have told the officer he had a gun on him. He wouldn't throw away the element of surprise. I can't speak for Castile, but he was probably reaching for his wallet.

The officer was charged with manslaughter. The prosecution's case against the officer was an uphill battle. In criminal court, you need to prove beyond a reasonable doubt that the crime was committed. I like the idea that the prosecution must prove that there is a 95% chance that the crime was committed. Of course, that means that all the defense needs to do is put enough doubt in the prosecution's case so that the jury is less than 95% certain. The jury ultimately found the officer not guilty of manslaughter.

The family then sued the city for wrongful death. In civil court, the circumstances are more balanced for the plaintiff. Instead of having to prove 95% certainty, the plaintiff only needs to prove roughly 50% certainty. The family was in a good position to win the civil suit, and so the city settled for three million dollars. At least the family got some justice in the process.

This was a big story at the time. And I won't knock news organizations for asking tough questions or investigating records, as long as the story is told in a way that would lead to an informed and rational public. CBS news put their own spin on the story. They had a segment that showed Castile's girlfriend and her daughter in the back of a squad car.[125] Castile's girlfriend was distraught after what had happened. She was angry and using foul language. The daughter said, "Mom, please stop cussing and screaming 'cause I don't want you to get shooted... I can keep you safe."

Does that add any new information to the story? Is that story meant to give the viewer new information? No, it's not. That story was designed to evoke an emotional response from the audience. And likely to stoke racial tensions in the U.S.

And this is not a left versus right issue. In 2023, *Fox News* settled a defamation lawsuit with Dominion Voting Systems. The lawsuit was due to *Fox News* pushing the idea that Dominion Voting Systems were involved in voting fraud that cost Donald Trump the 2020 presidential election. Many *Fox News* hosts including Sean Hannity, Tucker Carlson, and Laura Ingraham were skeptical about these voter fraud claims when they first surfaced. However, upper management at Fox did not want to risk alienating their audience. After all, a large portion of *Fox News* viewers are Republicans who voted for Trump.

*Fox News* and its hosts were willing to push a story that they didn't believe so that they could appease their audience. Instead of giving their audience the truth, they gave them lies that reeked of confirmation bias. According to the *New York Times*, "Fox News chief executive Suzanne Scott warned her colleagues against running fact-checking segments by the network's own reporters debunking lies about election fraud, even as it gave such bogus claims acres of prime real estate."[126]

Just as outlets like CNN had their reputations tarnished, *Fox News* deserves the stain on its credibility. Paying nearly $800 million in damages is just an additional price it pays for selling out.

I mentioned Andrew Klavan in the introduction of this book. On one of his shows, he talked about the media and its bias. He said, "We're not getting good stories. We're stuck in a lie. In a twisted distorted story and it's driving us insane and it's driving us apart. The people in this country could get together...I still believe this, the people in this country could get together. The people in this country could debate; we could pass laws that we all are a little bit dissatisfied with and a little bit satisfied with. We could get better people in office than either Joe Biden or Donald Trump, if people would stop lying to us ... they're telling us an untrue story, and that distorts everything."[127]

Speaking of Donald Trump and Joe Biden: I am writing this in January of 2024. At the moment, it seems that these two superannuated mediocrities will be the presidential candidates in the 2024 election cycle. As I mentioned back in Chapter 2, the United States has a massive debt problem. And if there is anything that will cause a collapse in American society, it will be the fiscal collapse under the weight of government debt.

As I showed in Chapter two, most of the economic gains made in the last fifteen years are false gains. You can talk about record high stock markets and GDP recovery; but what happens when the U.S. dollar is worthless due to hyperinflation? Or if the United States can no longer find suckers to buy their government bonds?

If we had leaders who were willing to take on the issue of the U.S. debt, I would say that America may actually survive. Unfortunately, almost every American politician is content to kick the can down the road. And those that are willing to tackle the issue do not hold any prominence. All while government spending and compound interest continues to increase the debt.

Speaking of elections, America seems to be more divided than ever. There is at least some truth to that. But, I also believe that you could find enough common ground that could satisfy most Americans. You'd be amazed at what a little good faith conversation could do. I once worked with a woman who was my political opposite. She was a lesbian and a woman who was far left of center. These days, you would have expected my inner *Fox News* and her inner CNN to collide and create a nuclear explosion.

But we talked like two normal adults. We listened to each other, respected each other's opinions, and tried to understand where we were both coming from. We ultimately agreed on world domination and to rule the world together. Man, our subjects are going to be getting some real mixed messages.

In everyday reality I don't think that our divisions are as wide as they appear. The *Washington Post* ran an article about a preacher in New Orleans named Isaiah Stewart.[129] The article is about Stewart being more than a pastor; he also helps people with firearm safety, firearm effectiveness, and getting concealed carry permits. As a licensed firearms instructor, Stewart wanted to help other black people have the means to protect themselves from criminals in New Orleans.

The best part of the story is around the middle of the article. Before Stewart was a firearms instructor, he felt like he needed to practice his shooting skills. He went to a local firing range. Stewart was the only black man there. Even though he appeared to be like a fish out of water, he practiced shooting anyway. During that session, Stewart was approached by a white man wearing a jacket with confederate flag patches on it. Stewart noticed the approaching figure and prepared for confrontation. Once he got to Stewart, the white man with the confederate flag on his jacket gave Stewart some advice on his form. Stewart said, "I realized that this was kind of breaking racial barriers. This White guy talking to a Black guy about guns."

This gives the idea that maybe we are not as divided and hateful toward each other as it appears. But much of the division that is taking America down is being sown by American politicians and media outlets. Joe Biden showed this when he gave a speech in front of Independence Hall in 2022. During the speech, he warned about the dangers of Donald Trump and "MAGA republicans," saying that "Donald Trump and MAGA republicans represent an extremism that threatens the very foundations of our republic." Now Biden did say that he didn't mean all republicans when discussing MAGA extremists. So, what makes a MAGA extremist?

Well according to Biden, "MAGA forces are determined take this country backwards. Backwards to an America where there is no right to choose, no right to privacy, no right to contraception, [and] no right to marry who you love."[128] So, if you are against abortion, you're a MAGA extremist. Being a prolife conservative, I guess I'm a right-wing extremist. Beware of my power. Catholics aren't big on birth control and other forms of contraception. You can add them to the list of MAGA extremists. And if you are not in favor of gay marriage, well chances are you were one of the January 6th insurrectionists.

The point is that for both corporate media and politicians, there are incentives to create divisive narratives. And the incentives are simple: money and power.

Politicians know they can get reelected easier when they paint the other side as evil. And it is not like the American right wing is innocent of this either. They are just as quick to indulge in fearmongering so they can appeal to conservative Americans.

Corporate media can get attention-grabbing headlines, so that they can get more clicks and add revenue. All the while America continues to decline further and further.

I know that this book is not the most uplifting and inspiring book. Unless you are one of those people who despise America, most people who read this book will probably feel sad or angry about America's eventual collapse. If you are one of those who despise America, I am glad that I could make you smile. I hope the post-American world is the utopia that you think it will be.

For the rest of us, it's sad to face the idea that the United States will fall and not just because life will get a lot harder for the average American. Life will become harder for nearly everyone in the world. The United States has used its large navy to ensure that countries can engage in global trade without fear of piracy. That has allowed countries to flourish through mutually beneficial trade. What happens when the United States can no longer afford to secure the oceans?

People will have fewer goods available to them at higher costs. Just because something says "made in USA" doesn't mean that the United States has everything necessary to manufacture that item. Raw materials and intermediate goods are imported to complete the final good. And the new hegemon is probably not going to be as charitable in global freedom and protection as the United States.

But the story of America will end. That is inevitable. Nothing lasts forever. Our bodies age, break down, and turn to dust. Like the human body, castles and kingdoms rise and crumble through the ages. But there is the concept of something after death that can give hope. Muslims, Jews, and Christians have the idea of Heaven and Hell, and the idea that something bigger and possibly better awaits us.

The concept of something after death doesn't have to be religious. The memory and legacy of nations persists throughout history. Look at the legacy of the Roman Empire. That society continued to influence the world long after the fall of Rome either through philosophy, mathematics, technological innovations, or historical lessons. The Roman Empire continues to live on in the thoughts of men. I probably think of the Roman Empire at least twice a week.

The same could be true for the United States. While it is uncertain how the United States will fall, there are plenty of lessons for future nations to learn from our mistakes.

Ensure that your society is based on objective reality. Objective standards and facts work as a medium for all of society. Don't allow your society to fall victim to subjective standards that conflict with each other.

Keep your institutions efficient and trustworthy. Maintain strict rules and responsibilities for these institutions. Society does not lose trust in institutions for no reason. Corrupt and self-serving institutions will destroy their own credibility. Remember that institutions exist to serve.

Be the best parent you can be. Parenting is not an easy job, but it is most necessary for the survival of our species. Invest time and effort in your children.

Stay away from authoritarianism. The human heart has a burning desire to be free. When tyrants lose their power, they tend to find themselves without a head.

Don't lie to young people about the world. Let them know what they can expect from their fellow man and what they should strive for. Avoid comforting and well-meaning lies. It will only lead to confusion and resentment.

Maintain a high standard for individuals in society. Give no attention to those that are engaging in a race to the bottom. If enough people in society race to the bottom, society will find itself feeding on rats in a basement. And do not let your people fall prey to moral relativism.

Don't let men fall into despair. Men will build monuments and fight wars for those they care about. Don't let society brand them as "toxic."

Remind people that there is more to society than themselves. Society starts with the individual, but it doesn't end there. Other people make life worth living; don't let vanity ruin that.

Beware the parasites in your society. They will consistently take from your society at the expense of others. And they will bring harm to your society. Remember: fleas and ticks bring bubonic plague and Lyme disease with them.

Let people know that actions have consequences. If people break laws and harm others, don't let them get away with it. Ensure that your society has a sense of justice.

Remind people that there is more to society than themselves. Society starts with the individual, but it doesn't end there. Other people make life worth living; don't let vanity ruin that.

These are lessons that future societies can learn after America dies. Future societies can learn from our mistakes. They can be better than us. Take on our strengths and improve our weaknesses. I like to think that one day, long after the fall of America, countries will look at our nation as a model for theirs. Maybe they can build a society that fully lives up to the American ideals—a society that seeks the protection of the individual. Just because America falls doesn't mean its long legacy of confidence, humanitarianism, and global innovation has to end.

# Works Cited

1. Merriam-Webster, March 27, 2023 https://www.merriam-webster.com/dictionary/objective

2. Brenan, Megan. "Americans' Trust In Media Remains Near Record Low". Gallup. https://news.gallup.com/poll/403166/americans-trust-media-remains-near-record-low.aspx

3. Sheffield, Rachel and Rector, Robert. "The War on Poverty After 50 Years". Heritage. September 15, 2014 https://www.heritage.org/poverty-and-inequality/report/the-war-poverty-after-50-years

4. "Percent of people in poverty". USA Facts. 2023. https://usafacts.org/data/topics/people-society/poverty/poverty-measures/poverty-rate-of-all-persons/

5. "Monthly Budget Review: Summary for Fiscal Year 2021" Congressional Budget Office. July 2021. https://www.cbo.gov/publication/57539/html

6. "Debt". USA Facts. 2023. https://usafacts.org/data/topics/government-finances/debt/

7. Silver, Caleb. "Over 10 Years Later, Lessons From the 2008 Financial Crisis". Investopedia. December 2, 2022. https://www.investopedia.com/news/10-years-later-lessons-financial-crisis/#citation-6

8. "What is the national deficit?" Fiscaldata.Treasury.Gov. October 2022. https://fiscaldata.treasury.gov/americas-finance-guide/national-deficit/

9. "The Budget and Economic Outlook: 2023 to 2033". Congressional Budget Office. November, 2022 https://www.cbo.gov/publication/58946#_idTextAnchor007

10. "Gross Domestic Product". Saint Louis FED. March 30, 2023. https://fred.stlouisfed.org/series/GDP/#0

11. "Chapter 4: Single Mothers" Pew Research. May 29, 2013. https://www.pewresearch.org/social-trends/2013/05/29/chapter-4-single-mothers/

12. Curtin, Sally. "Marriage Rates in the United States, 1900–2018". CDC. April 29, 2020 https://www.cdc.gov/nchs/data/hestat/marriage_rate_2018/marriage_rate_2018.htm

13. Kerr, Emma and Wood Sarah. "A Look at College Tuition Growth Over 20 Years". USA News. September 13, 2022 https://www.usnews.com/education/best-colleges/paying-for-college/articles/see-20-years-of-tuition-growth-at-national-universities

14. "36 Shocking Statistics on Fatherless Homes". Lifeisbeautiful.org. October 4, 2018. https://lifeisbeautiful.org/statistics-on-fatherless-homes/

15. C.R.S. 24-34-601. March 3, 2023. https://advance.lexis.com/documentpage/?pdmfid=1000516&crid=d2976049-ce81-43d0-b165-56ca93e0bce8&config=014FJAAyNGJkY2Y4Zi1mNjgyLTRkN2YtYmE4OS03NTYzNzYzOTg0OGEKAFBvZENhdGFsb2d592qv2Kywlf8caKqYROP5&pddocfullpath=%2fshared%2fdocument%2fstatutes-legislation%2furn%3acontentItem%3a630C-HY93-CH1B-T0S7-00008-00&pdcontentcomponentid=234176&pdteaserkey=sr0&pditab=allpods&ecomp=8s65kkk&earg=sr0&prid=6d8b9003-3678-4681-80cd-8079fbc26057

16. "Constitution of the United States". Congress.gov. https://constitution.congress.gov/constitution/amendment-14/

17. Blakemore, Erin. "How the Hitler Youth Turned a Generation of Kids Into Nazis." History. August 29, 2018. https://www.history.com/news/how-the-hitler-youth-turned-a-generation-of-kids-into-nazis

18. [Blaze TV]. (March 1, 2023) YouTube. "11-Year-Old SILENCES School Board As He Reads From DISTURBING Book Found In School Library". https://www.youtube.com/watch?v=CkgU0ZtKUxg

19. Nelson, Joshua. "1-year-old rips sexually explicit material in his Maine middle school: 'The librarian asked if I wanted more'" Fox News. February 28, 2023. https://www.foxnews.com/media/11-year-old-speaks-out-against-pornographic-content-maine-middle-school-admin-should-be-prosecuted

20. "CS/CS/HB 1557 — Parental Rights in Education" The Florida Senate. 2022. https://www.flsenate.gov/Committees/BillSummaries/2022/html/2825

21. "Florida Rights in Education" Bill. Florida Legislature. https://www.flsenate.gov/Session/Bill/2022/1557/BillText/er/PDF

22. "A Message From the Gay Community." Genuis.com July 1, 2021. https://genius.com/San-francisco-gay-mens-chorus-a-message-from-the-gay-community-lyrics

23. Duffin, Erin. "Estimated median age of Americans at their first wedding in the United States from 1998 to 2021, by sex." Statistica.com. October 12, 2022. https://www.statista.com/statistics/371933/median-age-of-us-americans-at-their-first-wedding/#:~:text=In%202021%2C%20the%20median%20age%20for%20the%20first,increasing%20for%20both%20men%20and%20women%20since%201998

24. Rudder, Christopher. "Dataclysm: Who We Are". Crown. September 9, 2014.

25. Tomassi, Rollo. "The Rational Male – Preventive Medicine" Counterflow Media. March 7, 2015.

26. Pargin, Jason. "6 Harsh Truths That Will Make You a Better Person". Cracked.com. December 17, 2012 https://www.cracked.com/blog/6-harsh-truths-that-will-make-you-better-person

27. Bellis, M and Hughs, K and Hughs, S and Ashton J. "Measuring paternal discrepancy and its public health consequences." National Library of Medicine. September 2005. https://www.ncbi.nlm.nih.gov/pmc/articles/PMC1733152/

28. "Rise of the SHEconomy" Morgan Stanley. September 23, 2019. https://www.morganstanley.com/ideas/womens-impact-on-the-economy

29. "Narcissistic Personality Disorder". Helpguide.org. March 28, 2023. https://www.helpguide.org/articles/mental-disorders/narcissistic-personality-disorder.htm

30. [Timcast IRL]. (February 3, 2023). "Virginia REFUSES To Ban Child Sex Changes, Jeff Younger Joins To Discuss His Story". YouTube. https://www.youtube.com/watch?v=Dc5mDUSIFx4

31. Grossman, Hannah. "New York teacher 'forced' and 'manipulated' 5th-grader to become transgender, causing suicidal ideation: suit". Fox News. February

28,2023. https://www.foxnews.com/media/new-york-teacher-forced-manipulated-5th-grader-become-transgender-causing-suicidal-ideation-suit

32. Reed, Jamie. "I Thought I Was Saving Trans Kids. Now I'm Blowing the Whistle.". The Free Press. February 9, 2023. https://www.thefp.com/p/i-thought-i-was-saving-trans-kids

33. Prestigiacomo, Amanda. "'Huge Money Maker': Video Reveals Vanderbilt's Shocking Gender 'Care,' Threats Against Dissenting Doctors". Dailywire. September 20 ,2022. https://www.dailywire.com/news/huge-money-maker-video-reveals-vanderbilts-shocking-gender-care-threats-against-dissenting-doctors

34. [Channel 4 Entertainment]. "Heartbreaking Moment When Kids Learn About White Privilege | The School That Tried to End Racism". YouTube. June 30, 2020. https://www.youtube.com/watch?v=1I3wJ7pJUjg

35. Evon, Dan. "Hillary Clinton and the Victims of War". Snopes. December 30, 2015. https://www.snopes.com/fact-check/hillary-clinton-victims-of-war/

36. [Steve Harvey Show] " Can A Marriage Be 50/50?". YouTube. April 12 ,2018. https://www.youtube.com/watch?v=O5Ie3nqHHA0

37. Male Labor Force Participation Rate. Bureau of Labor Statistics. March 25, 2023. https://data.bls.gov/pdq/SurveyOutputServlet

38. Kube, Courtney and Boigon, Molly. "Every branch of the military is struggling to make its 2022 recruiting goals, officials say". NBC News. June 27, 2022. https://www.nbcnews.com/news/military/every-branch-us-military-struggling-meet-2022-recruiting-goals-officia-rcna35078

39. "Suicide Data and Statistics". Center For Disease Control and Prevention. January 9, 2023. https://www.cdc.gov/suicide/suicide-data-statistics.html

40. "How Many Died in the American Civil War?" Bob Zeller. History. January 6, 2022. https://www.history.com/news/American-civil-war-deaths

41. "Declaration of Independence: A Transcription". NationalArchives.gov. https://www.archives.gov/founding-docs/declaration-transcript

42. "Leftist political commentator Hasan Piker faces criticism for buying a nearly $3 million home in Los Angeles County". Steven Asarch. Insider.

August 23, 2021. https://www.insider.com/hasan-piker-house-twitch-streamer-criticized-los-angeles-2021-8

43. "Modest Declines in Positive Views of 'Socialism' and 'Capitalism' in U.S." Pew Research Center. September 19, 2022. https://www.pewresearch.org/politics/2022/09/19/modest-declines-in-positive-views-of-socialism-and-capitalism-in-u-s/

44. "UK woman arrested a second time for 'offense' of silently praying outside abortion clinic: 'This isn't 1984'". Tietz, Kendall. March 7, 2023. Fox News. https://www.foxnews.com/media/uk-woman-arrested-second-time-offense-silently-praying-outside-abortion-clinic

45. "Taiwan's dominance of the chip industry makes it more important" The Economist. May 6, 2023. https://www.economist.com/special-report/2023/03/06/taiwans-dominance-of-the-chip-industry-makes-it-more-important

46. "Seattle Schools Propose to Teach That Math Education Is Racist—Will California Be Far Behind?" Ohanian, Lee. Hoover Institution. October 29, 2019. https://www.hoover.org/research/seattle-schools-propose-teach-math-education-racist-will-california-be-far-behindseattle

47. [John Stossel]. (March 21, 2023) "Diversity, Equity & Inclusion: DEI Training's Unintended Consequences." YouTube. https://www.youtube.com/watch?v=D2KX8wXzc78

48. "Trans woman is cleared of flashing her penis at three women using Ohio YMCA after judge ruled she's too FAT for her genitals to be visible". James, Emma. Daily Mail. May 6, 2023. https://www.dailymail.co.uk/news/article-12054769/Trans-woman-cleared-flashing-penis-YMCA-shes-FAT-genitals-visible.html

49. "Ana Kasparian doubles down after bashing trans-inclusive term 'birthing persons' as 'degrading' to women". Parks, Kristine and Chasmar, Jessica. New York Post. April 12, 2023.

50. "The dad who gave birth: 'Being pregnant doesn't change me being a trans man'". Hattenstone, Simon. April 20, 2019. https://www.theguardian.com/society/2019/apr/20/the-dad-who-gave-birth-pregnant-trans-freddy-mcconnell

51. "When the State Comes for Your Kids. Social workers, youth shelters, and the threat to parents' rights" Shrier, Abigail. City Journal. June 08, 2021. https://www.city-journal.org/article/when-the-state-comes-for-your-kids

52. "Woman who dreamed about being blind had DRAIN CLEANER poured in her eyes by a sympathetic psychologist to fulfil her lifelong wish – and now she's never been happier". Pickles, Kate. Daily Mail. October 1, 2015. https://www.dailymail.co.uk/health/article-3256029/Woman-dreamed-blind-DRAIN-CLEANER-poured-eyes-fulfil-lifelong-wish-says-happier-ever.html

53. "About 5% of young adults in the U.S. say their gender is different from their sex assigned at birth". Brown, Anna. Pew Research. June 7 , 2022. https://www.pewresearch.org/short-reads/2022/06/07/about-5-of-young-adults-in-the-u-s-say-their-gender-is-different-from-their-sex-assigned-at-birth/

54. "US regulator cites 'terrible' risk management for Silicon Valley Bank failure". Schroeder, Pete and Lang, Hannah. Rueters. March 28, 2023. https://www.reuters.com/markets/us/us-regulators-face-sharp-questions-congress-over-bank-collapses-2023-03-28/

55. "Diversity, Equity and Inclusion". Silicon Valley Bank. January 2022. https://www.svb.com/globalassets/library/uploadedfiles/dei-at-svb-january-2022.pdf

56. "When Women Earn More Than Their Husbands." University of Chicago Booth School of Business. February 18, 2013. https://www.chicagobooth.edu/media-relations-and-communications/press-releases/when-women-earn-more-than-their-husbands

57. "Marital status and suicide in the National Longitudinal Mortality Study". Kposowa, Augustine. University of California, Riverside, USA. August 12, 1999. https://www.ncbi.nlm.nih.gov/pmc/articles/PMC1731658/pdf/v054p00254.pdf

58. "Story of mother sentenced to jail for enrolling child in different district resurfaced amid college scandal". Daughtery, Owen. March 14, 2019. The Hill. https://thehill.com/blogs/blog-briefing-room/news/434051-story-of-mother-sentenced-to-jail-for-enrolling-child-in/

59. "Teachers Unions Are More Powerful Than You Realize—but That May Be Changing". McDonald, Kerry. Cato Institute. August 31, 2020. https://www.cato.org/commentary/teachers-unions-are-more-powerful-you-realize-may-be-changing

60. "Summary (Teachers Unions)". March 20, 2023. OpenSecrets. https://www.opensecrets.org/industries/indus.php?ind=L1300

61. "Average Cost of College by Year". Hanson, Melanie. Education Data Initiative. January 9, 2022. https://educationdata.org/average-cost-of-college-by-year

62. "TULANE UNIVERSITY ACADEMIC YEAR 2017-2018 FULL-TIME UNDERGRADUATE TUITION AND FEES TUITION AND MANDATORY FEES". Tulane University. https://studentaccounts.tulane.edu/sites/default/files/2017-2018_Full_Time_UG_costs.pdf

63. "TOPS OPH ANNUAL AWARD AMOUNTS FOR 2022-23". TOPS website. https://mylosfa.la.gov/wp-content/uploads/Current-Year-TOPS-Funding.pdf

64. "Income Share Agreements: What Are They, and How Do They Work?". Lane, Ryan and Beresford, Colin. Nerd Wallet. October 26, 2021. https://www.nerdwallet.com/article/loans/student-loans/income-share-agreements-what-students-should-know-before-borrowing

65. "Jazz Jennings: When I First Knew I Was Transgender." Jennings, Jazz. Time. May 31, 2016. https://time.com/4350574/jazz-jennings-transgender/

66. "Effects of domestic violence on children". U.S. Department of Health and Human Services/ Office on Women's Health. February 15, 2021. https://www.womenshealth.gov/relationships-and-safety/domestic-violence/effects-domestic-violence-children

67. "U.S. has world's highest rate of children living in single-parent households". Kramer, Stephanie. Pew Research. DECEMBER 12, 2019. https://www.pewresearch.org/short-reads/2019/12/12/u-s-children-more-likely-than-children-in-other-countries-to-live-with-just-one-parent/

68. "Revealing Divorce Statistics In 2023". Bieber, Christy. Forbes Advisor. May 4, 2023. https://www.forbes.com/advisor/legal/divorce/divorce-statistics/

69. "Gupta tells Joe Rogan CNN shouldn't have called ivermectin 'horse dewormer'". Mastrangelo, Dominick. The Hill. October 14, 2021 https://thehill.com/homenews/media/576723-gupta-tells-joe-rogan-cnn-shouldn't-have-called-ivermectin-horse-dewormer/

70. "Censorship or misinformation? DeSantis and YouTube spar over COVID roundtable takedown". Knight, Victoria. Politifact. April 21,2021. https://www.politifact.com/article/2021/apr/21/censorship-or-misinformation-desantis-and-youtube-/

71. "Provisional Mortality Data — United States, 2020". Center For Disease Control and Prevention. March 7, 2023. https://www.cdc.gov/mmwr/volumes/70/wr/mm7014e1.htm

72. "Man dies after taking chloroquine in an attempt to prevent coronavirus". Edwards, Erica and Hillyard, Vaughn. March 23, 2020. NBC News. https://www.nbcnews.com/health/health-news/man-dies-after-ingesting-chloroquine-attempt-prevent-coronavirus-n1167166

73. "CNN's Don Lemon rips stay-at-home protesters for 'complaining that they don't have haircuts'". Wulfsohn, Joseph. Fox News. April 20, 2020. https://www.foxnews.com/media/cnn-don-lemon-stay-at-home-protestors-haircuts

74. "My Husband Won't Take His Mask Off—Even for Sex" ADVICE BY SLATE STAFF. Slate. MAY 27, 2021. https://slate.com/human-interest/2021/05/dear-prudence-mask-coronavirus-fear-sex.html

75. "Fact Sheet: Biden Administration Announces Details of Two Major Vaccination Policies". The White House. November 04, 2021. https://www.whitehouse.gov/briefing-room/statements-releases/2021/11/04/fact-sheet-biden-administration-announces-details-of-two-major-vaccination-policies/

76. "Supreme Court blocks Biden Covid vaccine mandate for businesses, allows health-care worker rule." Breuninger, Kevin and Kimball, Spencer. CNBC. January 13, 2022. https://www.cnbc.com/2022/01/13/supreme-court-ruling-biden-covid-vaccine-mandates.html#:~:text=Investing%20Club-,Supreme%20Court%20blocks%20Biden%20Covid%20vaccine%20mandate%20for,allows%20health%2

Dcare%20worker%20rule&text=The%20Supreme%20Court%20on%20Thursday,requirements%20for%20large%20private%20companies.

77. [The Quartering] (November 8, 2022) "This Teacher Stalks Students." YouTube. https://www.youtube.com/shorts/XxMlOL-CzZc

78. "Terry McAuliffe's War on Parents". The editors. National Review. October 1, 2021. https://www.nationalreview.com/2021/10/terry-mcauliffes-war-on-parents/#:~:text=%E2%80%9CI%20believe%20parents%20should%20be,schools%20what%20they%20should%20teach.%E2%80%9D

79. "What to Know About Florida's New 'Don't Say Gay' Rule That Bans Discussion of Gender for All Students". Burga, Solcyre. TIME. April 20, 2023.

80. "Florida's governor signs controversial law opponents dubbed 'Don't Say Gay'". Diaz, Jaclyn. NPR. March 28, 2022. https://www.npr.org/2022/03/28/1089221657/don't-say-gay-florida-desantis

81. "The Dangerous Consequences of Florida's "Don't Say Gay" Bill on LGBTQ+ Youth in Florida". Johnson, Meredith. (No date given) Georgetown Law. https://www.law.georgetown.edu/gender-journal/online/volume-xxiii-online/the-dangerous-consequences-of-floridas-don't-say-gay-bill-on-lgbtq-youth-in-florida/

82. "Disney Executive Producer Admits to 'Gay Agenda,' 'Adding Queerness' Wherever She Could." Downey, Caroline. March 29, 2022. National Review. https://www.nationalreview.com/news/Disney-executive-producer-admits-to-gay-agenda-adding-queerness-wherever-she-could/

83. "'Blue's Clues' teams up with drag queen Nina West for Pride Month." Boniello, Kathianne. New York Post. May 29, 2021. https://nypost.com/2021/05/29/blues-clues-teams-up-with-drag-queen-nina-west-for-pride-month/

84. "Constitution of the United States: Tenth Amendment." Constitution Annotated. https://constitution.congress.gov/constitution/amendment-10/

85. "Graham Introduces Legislation to Protect Unborn Children, Bring U.S. Abortion Policy in Line with Other Developed Nations." Sep 13 2022. Lindsey Graham Press Release.

https://www.lgraham.senate.gov/public/index.cfm/2022/9/graham-introduces-legislation-to-protect-unborn-children-bring-u-s-abortion-policy-in-line-with-other-developed-nations

86. "Female Fertility By Age". Stanneck, Becca. Forbes Health. October 27, 2022. https://www.forbes.com/health/family/female-fertility-by-age/

87. Carter, G. L., et al. The Dark Triad personality: Attractiveness to women. Personality and Individual Differences (2013), http://dx.doi.org/10.1016/j.paid.2013.08.021

88. "Single-Parent Families Rise Dramatically". Rich, Spencer. The Washington Post. May 3, 1982. https://www.washingtonpost.com/archive/politics/1982/05/03/single-parent-families-rise-dramatically/cc4afac4-2764-419e-8bda-66f14bad3dd0/

89. "Top Deal-Breakers on Dating Apps." Alexander. Date Psychology. April 25, 2023. https://datepsychology.com/top-deal-breakers-on-dating-apps/#comments

90. "Study reveals unhealthy attraction to thin women" Macquarie University. June 6, 2016. https://www.mq.edu.au/thisweek/2016/06/06/body-beautiful-healthy-versus-thin/

91. "Fertility Rate, Total for the United States." St. Louis FED. May 9, 2023 https://fred.stlouisfed.org/series/SPDYNTFRTINUSA

92. "Lizzo Says She 'Is the Beauty Standard,' Calls out Discourse Around Her Body" Ward, Fiona. Glamour. April 19, 2023. https://www.glamour.com/story/lizzo-says-she-is-the-beauty-standard-calls-out-discourse-around-her-body

93. "Megan Fox has a blood drinking ritual with Machine Gun Kelly and thinks social media is 'sinister'". Respers, Lisa. CNN. April 27, 2022. https://www.cnn.com/2022/04/27/entertainment/megan-fox-machine-gun-blood/index.html

94. "Elon Musk slams Sam Smith's 'Satan' Grammy performance: 'End of days'". Lefroy, Emily. New York Post. February 7, 2023. https://nypost.com/2023/02/07/elon-musk-slams-sam-smiths-satan-grammy-performance-end-of-days/

95. "How the geography of U.S. poverty has shifted since 1960." Krogstad, Jens. Pew Research. September 15,

2015. https://www.pewresearch.org/short-reads/2015/09/10/how-the-geography-of-u-s-poverty-has-shifted-since-1960/

96. "San Francisco City and County." Bay Area Census. http://www.bayareacensus.ca.gov/counties/SanFranciscoCounty50.htm

97. "Income of Families and Persons in the United States: 1949". United States Census Bureau. February 18, 1951. https://www.census.gov/library/publications/1951/demo/p60-007.html#:~:text=The%20income%20of%20the%20average,years%20of%201944%20and%201945.

98. "QuickFacts San Francisco city, California" United States Census Bureau. https://www.census.gov/quickfacts/sanfranciscocitycalifornia

99. "Income in the United States: 2021." Semega, Jessica and Kollar, Melissa. United States Census Bureau. September 13, 2022. https://www.census.gov/library/publications/2022/demo/p60-276.html

100. "People are pooping more than ever on the streets of San Francisco". Gibert, Ben. Insider. Apr 18, 2019. https://www.businessinsider.com/san-francisco-human-poop-problem-2019-4

101. "City Hall hands out 4.45 million syringes each year, says report". Brinklow, Adam. Curbed San Francisco. May 9, 2018. https://sf.curbed.com/2018/5/9/17336090/san-francisco-needles-syringes-exchange-numbers-sf

102. "Nancy Pelosi guest stars on drag queen TV show." Ferrechio, Susan. The Washington Times. June 10, 2022. https://www.washingtontimes.com/news/2022/jun/10/nancy-pelosi-guest-star-rupaul-drag-queen-show/

103. "Pennsylvania School Hosts Drag Show for Kids Without Parent's Permission". Arnold, Sarah. Townhall. May 12, 2022. https://townhall.com/tipsheet/saraharnold/2022/05/12/Pennsylvania-school-is-in-hot-water-for-hosting-drag-show-for-kids-n2607149

104. Wang G, Djafarian K, Egedigwe CA, El Hamdouchi A, Ojiambo R, Ramuth H, Wallner-Liebmann SJ, Lackner S, Diouf A, Sauciuvenaite J, Hambly C, Vaanholt LM, Faries MD, Speakman JR. The relationship of female physical attractiveness to body fatness. PeerJ. 2015 Aug 25;3:e1155. Doi: 10.7717/peerj.1155. PMID: 26336638; PMCID: PMC4556148. https://www.ncbi.nlm.nih.gov/pmc/articles/PMC4556148/

105. "Defining Adult Overweight & Obesity". Center For Disease Control and Prevention. https://www.cdc.gov/obesity/basics/adult-defining.html

106. "Rebel Wilson and Adele say losing weight has made them happy. But some fans feel angry and 'betrayed.' Here's why." Greenfield, Beth. Yahoo. January 21, 2022. https://www.yahoo.com/lifestyle/rebel-wilson-adele-losing-weight-fans-angry-betrayed-192915875.html?fr=sycsrp_catchall

107. "Healthy Eating for a Healthy Weight." Center For Disease Control and Prevention. https://www.cdc.gov/healthyweight/healthy_eating/index.html

108. "Health Effects of Overweight and Obesity." Center For Disease Control and Prevention. https://www.cdc.gov/healthyweight/effects/index.html

109. "COUNTY ADULT ASSISTANCE PROGRAMS (CAAP) Apply for CAAP." San Francisco Human Services Agency. https://www.sfhsa.org/services/financial-assistance/county-adult-assistance-programs-caap/apply-caap

110. "Checking Your Eligibility". San Francisco Human Services Agency. https://www.sfhsa.org/services/food/calfresh/applying-calfresh/checking-your-eligibility

111. "CalFresh Data Dashboard." Department of Social Services. https://www.cdss.ca.gov/inforesources/data-portal/research-and-data/calfresh-data-dashboard

112. "Select a Medi-Cal Health Care Plan". San Francisco Human Services Agency. https://www.sfhsa.org/services/health/medi-cal/select-medi-cal-health-care-plan

113. [John Stossel]. (Sep 22, 2016). YouTube. "Freeloaders: Panhandling". https://www.youtube.com/watch?v=IhoiVnID8vY

114. "Did Kamala Harris Bail Out 'Violent Rioters' During George Floyd Protests?" Lee, Jessica. Snopes. February 16, 2021. https://www.snopes.com/fact-check/harris-protesters-bail/

115. "San Francisco car owners take drastic measures as break-ins skyrocket: 'I'm shocked'". Colton, Emma. Fox News. December 15, 2021. https://www.foxnews.com/us/san-francisco-residents-cars-open-windows-trunks-measures-combat-break-ins

116. "'Do As They Say': Minneapolis Police Tell Residents To 'Be Prepared To Give Up' Personal Belongings To Robbers". Brown, Jon. Daily Wire. https://www.dailywire.com/news/do-as-they-say-minneapolis-police-tell-residents-to-be-prepared-to-give-up-personal-belongings-to-robbers

117. "What Is Toxic Masculinity?" Vallie, Sarah. WebMD. November 11, 2022. https://www.webmd.com/sex-relationships/what-is-toxic-masculinity#:~:text=safer%2C%20healthier%20society.-,What%20Is%20Toxic%20Masculinity%3F,in%20itself%20is%20inherently%20bad

118. Supporting Women in Fire and EMS: The USFA Commitment. U.S Fire Administration. May 9, 2023. https://www.usfa.fema.gov/blog/ci-030321.html#:~:text=Women%20in%20fire%20and%20EMS%3A%20Learn%20about%20the%20professional%20development,at%20the%20National%20Fire%20Academy.&text=5%25%20of%20all%20career%20firefighters,volunteer%20fire%20service%20are%20women.

119. "For Valentine's Day, 5 facts about single Americans." Gelles-Watnick, Risa. Pew Research Center. February 8, 2023. https://www.pewresearch.org/short-reads/2023/02/08/for-valentines-day-5-facts-about-single-americans/

120. "Overweight & Obesity Statistics". National Institute of Diabetes and Digestive and Kidney Diseases. September 2021. https://www.niddk.nih.gov/health-information/health-statistics/overweight-obesity#:~:text=More%20women%20(11.5%25)%20than,60%20and%20older%20(5.8%25).

121. "Mental Illness". National Institute for Mental Health. March 2023. https://www.nimh.nih.gov/health/statistics/mental-illness

122. "Percentage of U.S. women with any or serious mental illness in the past year as of 2021, by age". Elflein, John. Statistica.com. Jan 16, 2023. https://www.statista.com/statistics/666374/mental-illness-in-the-past-year-among-us-women-by-age/

123. "Men going their own way: the rise of a toxic male separatist movement" Bates, Laura. The Guardian. August, 26 2020.

https://www.theguardian.com/lifeandstyle/2020/aug/26/men-going-their-own-way-the-toxic-male-separatist-movement-that-is-now-mainstream

124. Suicide. National Institute of Mental Health. May 2023. https://www.nimh.nih.gov/health/statistics/suicide#part_2558

125. [CBS Evening News] (June, 21 2017) YouTube. "New video from aftermath of Castile shooting shows girl's bravery". https://www.youtube.com/watch?v=cYZ2S_TsBu0

126. "Fox News settles blockbuster defamation lawsuit with Dominion Voting Systems." Yang, Mary and Folkenflik, David. New York Times. April 18, 2023. https://www.npr.org/2023/04/18/1170339114/fox-news-settles-blockbuster-defamation-lawsuit-with-dominion-voting-systems

127. [The Andrew Klavan Show] (May, 12 2023).Dailywire. " Ep. 1130 - Biden Corruption, Media Lies". https://www.dailywire.com/episode/ep-1130-biden-corruption-media-lies7

128. [6abc Philadelphia] (September 1, 2022) YouTube. "FULL SPEECH: Biden delivers address outside Independence Hall on 'extremist threat to democracy'" https://www.youtube.com/watch?v=XC-k-lhml4o

129. "Carrying a Bible and a gun, a pastor tends to an unsettled New Orleans." Bailey, Holly. Washington Post. May 12, 2023. https://www.washingtonpost.com/nation/2023/05/12/new-orleans-pastor-gun-violence-firearm-safety/

130. Murray, Charles. Coming Apart: the State of White America. The Crown Publishing Group. 01/29/2013.

131. "2020 Final Death Statistics: COVID-19 as an Underlying Cause of Death vs. Contributing Cause". CDC. January 7, 2022. https://www.cdc.gov/nchs/pressroom/podcasts/2022/20220107/20220107.htm

132. "SVB's Lack of Risk Officer Emerges as Focus in Fed Probe". Johnson, Katanga and Rosenblatt, Joel and Dolmetsch, Chris. Insurance Journal. March 15, 2023. https://www.insurancejournal.com/news/national/2023/03/15/712253.htm

133. "Charges Dropped Against Idaho Mother Arrested for Taking Kids to Playground During COVID Closure." Big Country News. Jan 5, 2023. https://www.bigcountrynewsconnection.com/idaho/charges-dropped-again

st-idaho-mother-arrested-for-taking-kids-to-playground-during-covid-closure/article_49ed4fca-8d41-11ed-8ea5-2354c02dedbd.html

134. "Nearly 6,000 US public schools hide child's gender status from parents". Christenson, Josh. New York Post. March 8, 2023. https://nypost.com/2023/03/08/us-public-schools-conceal-childs-gender-status-from-parents/

135. "Fatal Force" The Washington Post. Updated October 23,2023. https://www.washingtonpost.com/graphics/investigations/police-shootings-database/

136. [First Coast News] October 18, 2023. YouTube. "Dashcam footage shows deputy shoot Leonard Cure, Georgia man exonerated after 16 years in prison". https://www.youtube.com/watch?v=tGNIAozOIok

137. "2018 Crime in America." Criminal Justice Information Services Division. https://ucr.fbi.gov/crime-in-the-u.s/2018/crime-in-the-u.s.-2018/tables/table-43/#overview

138. "I slept with 300 people in a year — haters say I'm 'disgusting' but I feel empowered." Court, Andrew. New York Post. October 17, 2023. https://nypost.com/2023/10/17/i-slept-with-300-people-in-a-year-haters-say-im-disgusting-but-i-feel-empowered/

139. "Number of occupational injury deaths in the U.S. from 2003 to 2020, by gender." Statistica.com. Aug 1, 2023. https://www.statista.com/statistics/187127/number-of-occupational-injury-deaths-in-the-us-by-gender-since-2003/

140. "Adult Obesity Facts". CDC.gov. May 17, 2022. https://www.cdc.gov/obesity/data/adult.html#:~:text=From%201999%20%E2%80%932000%20through%202017%20%E2%80%93March%2020 20%2C%20US,of%20severe%20obesity%20increased%20from%204.7%25%20to%209.2%25.

141. "The Satanic Temple". thesatanictemple.com. Viewed on 12-26-2023. https://cdn.shopify.com/s/files/1/0428/0465/files/TST_Info_pamphlet_02-01.pdf?v=1658244397

142. "What we know about rape and sexual violence inflicted by Hamas during its terror attack on Israel". Kottasova, Ivana. CNN. December 7,

2023. https://edition.cnn.com/2023/12/06/middleeast/rape-sexual-violence-hamas-israel-what-we-know-intl/index.html

143. "Netanyahu's office releases horrifying images of infants murdered by Hamas." Spiro, Amy. The Times of Israel. 12 October 2023. https://www.timesofisrael.com/netanyahus-office-releases-horrifying-images-of-infants-murdered-by-hamas/

144. "Key Results -December". Harvard CAPS / Harris Poll. December 15, 2023. https://harvardharrispoll.com/wp-content/uploads/2023/12/HHP_Dec23_KeyResults.pdf

145. "Signs of a Narcissistic Sociopath". Jackson, Sean. Mentalhealth.com. Sep 14th 2023. https://www.mentalhealth.com/disorder/narcissistic-personality-disorder/signs-of-a-narcissistic-sociopath

146. "Harvard's Affirmative Action Rationale Is Bogus". Kenny Xu. City Journal. September 1, 2023. https://www.city-journal.org/article/harvards-affirmative-action-rationale-is-bogus

147. "How one college spends more than $30M on 241 DEI staffers ... and the damage it does to kids." McGuire, Steven. New York Post. Jan. 11, 2024. https://nypost.com/2024/01/11/opinion/dei-boondoggle-costs-us-millions-and-harms-students-it-claims-to-help/

148. [Shoe0nHead]. (Aug 7, 2023). YouTube. "The Male Loneliness Epidemic". https://www.youtube.com/watch?v=rQv8VuLpKN4

149. [Shoe0nHead]. (Sep 11, 2023). YouTube. "Men Deserve To Be Lonely!" Responding To Backlash Over 'The Male Loneliness Epidemic'". https://www.youtube.com/watch?v=qVKvEaokV6I&t=535s

150. [Dailywire+]. (Feb 10, 2020). YouTube. "Australian TV Show Shames Stay-at-Home Mom".

151. "CNN ridiculed for 'Fiery But Mostly Peaceful' caption with video of burning building in Kenosha". Choncha, Joe. 08/27/20. The Hill. 08/27/20. https://thehill.com/homenews/media/513902-cnn-ridiculed-for-fiery-but-mostly-peaceful-caption-with-video-of-burning/

www.ingramcontent.com/pod-product-compliance
Lightning Source LLC
Chambersburg PA
CBHW050242010526
44107CB00032B/1386/J